K. P. Daniels, June 13,

KU-515-669

BRUNEL
and his world

JOHN PUDNEY

BRUNEL
and his world

THAMES AND HUDSON
LONDON

Frontispiece: IKB at the Millwall
shipyards in 1857, during preparations for the launch of the *Great
Eastern.* A note in Brunel's hand-
writing on the back of this
photograph states: 'I asked Mr
Lenox to stand with me, but he
would not, so I alone am hung in
chains.'

© *1974 Thames and Hudson Ltd,
London*

Reprinted 1975

*All Rights Reserved. No part of this
publication may be reproduced or
transmitted in any form or by any means,
electronic or mechanical, including
photocopy, recording or any information
storage and retrieval system, without
permission in writing from the publisher.*

*Printed in Great Britain
by Jarrold and Sons Ltd, Norwich*

ISBN 0 500 13047 7

A portrait of Sir Marc Isambard Brunel (1769–1849) celebrating his most famous achievement, the Thames Tunnel. The son of Norman farmers, destined by his parents for the Church, he had served in the French Navy, taken American citizenship, and occupied the post of Chief Engineer of New York City before coming to England.

'I HAVE BEEN MAKING half a dozen boats lately, till I have worn my hands to pieces. I have also taken a plan of Hove, which is a very amusing job. I should be much obliged to you if you would ask papa (I hope he is quite well and hearty), whether he would lend me his long measure....' So went a letter home, written in 1820 from boarding-school at Hove, by Isambard Kingdom Brunel, aged fourteen.

No doubt 'papa', Marc Isambard Brunel, obliged, for he had been precocious too. As a young boy in his native France, after receiving his third lesson in trigonometry he had asked permission to measure the height of the spire of Rouen Cathedral with an instrument of his own devising.

It was indeed a case of like father, like son. The elder Brunel's teacher had been amazed to find that he had only to state once the propositions of Euclid for his pupil to understand them without explanation. Marc in turn had the satisfaction of seeing his son mastering Euclid at the age of six.

During this period of precipitous evolution, from sail to steam, from rutted turnpike highways to the iron railroads, from landed feudalism to the beginnings of modern democracy, there were generation gaps such as had never been seen before or since. Yet here and there were families favoured with exceptional continuity. As I. K. Brunel followed an eminent father, so Robert Stephenson, his contemporary, rival and friend, followed the renowned George Stephenson. Both second-generation men, they met the challenge of their century, blessed with talent and background. But their pioneering energies were such that they had worked themselves to death by the time they reached their mid fifties. They died young in a young man's world. Succeeding generations have often mistakenly regarded their age as stuffy, elderly, ponderous with whiskers and heavy watch-chains, a period of rigid morals, joylessness and harshly enforced conventions. Superficially there was some support for this conception: the social scene looked placid so long as it was not explored in depth. Progress from an agricultural to an industrial economy seemed stable and assured so long as the effects of intense competition and human exploitation were not too closely studied. In fact, the revolutionary changes, not only in material things but in human values, were moving so fast that it took men of quite exceptional quality to apprehend, mould and master the new energies which were abroad.

The history books have done less than justice to these men. While the names of politicians, battle-winners and empire-builders predominate, the innovators who fashioned and consolidated, who provided power and wealth and engineered the progress of the nineteenth century in Britain and elsewhere are curiously neglected.

Though their ideas were big, their world was small. These self-made men mingled freely with one another and with the wealthy, noble and royal who sustained privilege and tradition. With bitter rivalries went generous exchanges of advice and ideas. The arts and sciences were not aloof from one another. The Court was not aloof from either. The landed gentry soon discovered themselves as interested parties in the Industrial Revolution. The reign of Victoria was superficially class conscious, yet people of humble or unlikely origin kept breaking through, and the Establishment was sufficiently flexible to accommodate their energies and ideas. The Duke of Devonshire's gardener from Chatsworth, Joseph Paxton, designed the Crystal Palace, walked and talked with the Prince Consort, entered Parliament and was knighted. Henry Maudslay, who with his sons supplied so much of the engine-power for the achievements of the Brunels and other pioneers of the period, had started his working life filling cartridges in Woolwich Arsenal.

The younger Brunel benefited enormously from close association with his father, for Marc Isambard Brunel was a singular man by any

(*Above*) The moulders of the new age, the outstanding men of science in the early years of the nineteenth century, including Marc Isambard Brunel (second from left at table), Davies Gilbert, chief judge of the Clifton Bridge competition (at left, wearing sash), and Henry Maudslay (left, behind Brunel).

The unlikely and perilous future as it appeared to doubting eyes in 1837. Industrialization and steam-power ushered in an age of discovery without precedent and helped to create both the glories and the squalor of the Victorian world.

The leisure of the pampered rich – and their pampered pets – was often enjoyed at appalling human expense. To many earnest Victorians the poor constituted an invisible underworld, to be mined for wealth until the vein was exhausted.

One of a series of machines for the assembly-line production of naval blocks, invented by Marc Isambard. Upon these designs he pinned his hopes of fortune when he left New York for England in 1799. Manufactured by Maudslay, then beginning his own career as the greatest mechanic of the period, this apparatus established the elder Brunel's reputation in England.

standards. Born in the same year as Napoleon Bonaparte, 1769, he became an American citizen in his twenties and ended his days with a British knighthood bestowed by Queen Victoria. As a French naval officer under Louis XVI, he escaped from the Revolution to New York in 1793 and became Chief Engineer of New York City. Six years later he went to Britain with an invention for naval block-making machinery (his working model may still be seen in the National Maritime Museum, Greenwich), married Sophia Kingdom, settled eventually in Chelsea and flung himself into a succession of ventures, all creative but not all rewarding. His finances collapsed in 1821, when his son Isambard was fifteen, and he went as a debtor to King's Bench Prison for a short spell. The Duke of Wellington managed to persuade the authorities to grant him £5,000 to obtain his discharge on condition that he remain in England. On his release he was involved in an astonishing diversity of activities including a stocking-knitting machine, printing machinery and paddle-wheel marine propulsion. He designed bridges and docks and Liverpool's first floating landing-stage. He worked for the Government at Chatham and at Woolwich. Though he honoured his promise to remain based in Britain, he carried out works abroad. For the French Government he designed two suspension bridges for the Ile-de-Bourbon near Mauritius. For the Dutch Government he carried out ordnance work.

Not least among his preoccupations was the upbringing of his son whose education he kept entirely in his own hands until, at the age of nine, the boy was sent to Hove. At school there the boy demonstrated the uncanny mixture of insight and practical knowledge which he shared with his father. Once, he took bets that some buildings being constructed opposite the school would fall down; during the night the walls collapsed as he had predicted. His father in the same way had foretold the collapse of a newly erected store-shed at Deptford which was in ruins the following morning. After a single glance at the drawings of the first suspension bridge over the Seine in Paris the elder Brunel had pronounced its doom, and a few days later the bridge was down in the water.

Brunel memorial plaque, Portsea.

From Hove young Isambard continued an education singularly suited to his talents. When he was home from school his father kept him by his side so that he became familiar with an array of engineers, scientists and public men of the period. Marc for instance worked closely with Henry Maudslay the great engineer and founder of the most significant engineering works of the century – and Maudslay's pupils were to include such young men as Joseph Whitworth and James Nasmyth, almost exact contemporaries of young Isambard. Politicians and patrons such as the second Earl Spencer, First Lord of the Admiralty under Pitt, and later the Iron Duke were familiar figures.

Though Marc Isambard was Anglophile and intended that the future of his family should lie in Britain, he avoided the British system

His block-making machines accepted for manufacture by the Royal Navy, Marc Isambard married and settled near Portsmouth Dockyards where he was to supervise their installation. In Portsea his only son, Isambard Kingdom, was born in 1806.

To provide the best possible training for his career, IKB was sent at the age of fourteen to France to complete his formal education. At the Lycée Henri-Quatre in Paris (pictured here), he studied mathematics.

of education for his son. At the age of fourteen, young Isambard went to the College of Caen in Normandy, then to the Lycée Henri-Quatre in Paris, famous for its mathematics. Finally he was apprenticed to Abraham Louis Breguet, manufacturer of chronometers and scientific instruments. So famous was this school of horologists that graduates proudly described themselves for years after leaving him as 'Élève de Breguet'.

At seventeen young Isambard's formal education was finished and he entered his father's office, more qualified than most to share in the multifarious activities going on there, currently including designs for a suspension bridge over the Serpentine, swing bridges for Liverpool Docks and work for the Admiralty on the practical application of condensed gases.

The paternal office has been described as a homely little affair with only a single clerk to assist father and son during this period. There was not much money about, and home life by the river in Chelsea was cheerful though somewhat restricted to the eyes of a young man fresh from Paris. He had begun to write a journal and made a habit of confronting himself with his hopes, ambitions, anxieties and exasperations. An entry in February 1825, for instance, mentions 'Une dispute avec mon père, qui me menace de me donner un soufflet; je ne le souffrirai pas.' During the following month an entry reveals his uneasiness:

Projects are on foot for Fowey and Padstow Canal, and the Bermondsey Docks. I am preparing plans for South London Docks. In case my father should be named Engineer [of the Docks] I am busily engaged on the Gas Engine, and the project is likewise made for a canal across the Panama. Surely *one of these* may take place!

It may be curious at some future date to read the state we are in at present – I am most terribly pinched for money. Should receive barely enough next quarter to pay my debts, and am, at this moment, without a penny. We keep neither carriage, nor horse, nor footman, only two maidservants. I am looking forward with great anxiety to this gas engine – building castles in the air about steamboats going 15 miles per hour; going on a tour to Italy; being the first to go to the West Indies, and making a large fortune; building a house for myself, etc., etc. How much more likely it is that all this will turn out to nothing! that the Gas Engine, if it is good for anything, will only be tolerably good, and perhaps make us spend a good deal of money; that I should pass through life as most other people do, and that I should gradually forget my castles in the air, live in a small house, and at most, keep my gig. On the other side it may be much worse. My father may die, or the Tunnel may fail. . . .

The journal also lists some of the pleasures of the period. Young Isambard shared with his friend William Hawes the ownership of a 'funny', a light, clinker-built skulling-boat much favoured for rowing; and there were excursions for swimming at Greenwich and Richmond on summer evenings. It was fortunate that Isambard became a strong swimmer, for this saved his life during work on the project which for several years to come overshadowed their lives – the Thames Tunnel.

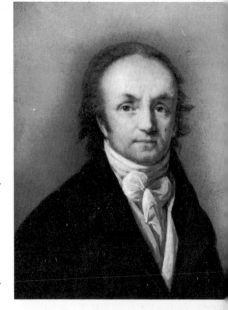

The final phase of IKB's continental education was an apprenticeship to the famous maker of chronometers and scientific instruments, Abraham Louis Breguet (1747–1823), widely regarded as the master craftsman in his field. Breguet was impressed by the young Brunel's inventiveness, and no doubt from him Brunel learned to respect and demand the highest standards of workmanship.

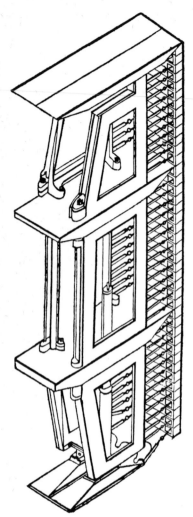

In spite of his other distractions the elder Brunel had come to regard the penetration of a tunnel beneath the Thames tideway as his personal destiny and incidentally his hope of making the fortune which was always eluding him. One of his early manifestos declared: 'We may soon anticipate a speedy and total change in the face of the maps of this great metropolis – in that portion of it which has hitherto presented nothing but swampy desert – namely the parish of Rotherhithe. . . . This parish will soon display a scene of activity that is not to be witnessed anywhere else.'

His obsession – for this is what it had become – rested materially upon a patent he had first taken out in 1818 for a tunnelling shield. This invention he owed to his formidable curiosity and to the fact that he never went anywhere without equipment for satisfying it, such as the magnifying glass in his waistcoat pocket.

In Chatham Dockyard, supervising work which included a short tunnel for the conveyance of timber, he noticed some keel timber which had been attacked by *teredo navalis*, the ship-worm which destroyed the Royal Navy's wooden walls more relentlessly than enemy cannon. Through the magnifying glass Marc Isambard studied the action of a living worm digging into the wood, grinding it into a nourishing meal, then excreting it to form the smooth lining of a tunnel in which the creature operated.

His tunnelling shield was a reproduction in iron of the mechanism of the ship-worm. Its basic form was an iron cylinder, propelled forward horizontally by jacks, enclosing miners working a cutting-edge, with more miners behind them lining the excavation with brick. This was modified and improved until it went into action as his Great Shield.

Characteristic of the age was the acceptance that the inventor needed also to be a lobbyist and businessman. The Brunels, as well as many

Though slow and laborious in its progress, the great tunnelling shield made an underwater tunnel through soft earth feasible for the first time in history. One frame contained three divisions; there were twelve such frames, each twenty-two feet high and about three feet wide, presenting thirty-six chambers in all.

The shield in action, seen through the already completed portions of the arches. The shield was manned by an élite corps of workers, selected by the elder Brunel.

other pioneers of their time, not only possessed immense self-confidence but shared an ability to work and think at all levels. Before forming his Thames Tunnel Company in 1824, Marc Isambard had canvassed businessmen, bankers, canal company directors and of course the Iron Duke himself.

Waited on the Duke of Wellington by appointment, the object of which was to have the plan of the mode of proceeding with the tunnel explained to him. His Grace made many very good observations and raised great objections; but after having explained to him my Plan and the expedients I had in reserve, His Grace appeared to be satisfied and to be disposed to subscribe.

With £160,000 capital subscribed, the company formed; and both Houses of Parliament having passed the Bill for its incorporation, the driving of the tunnel project began to materialize in 1824 when Marc Isambard gave up his office in the City and his home at Chelsea and moved with his family to Bridge Street, Blackfriars, to be near the scene of operations. He laid the first brick at Cow Court, Rotherhithe in March 1825 and young Isambard laid the second. It was significant that the beginning of the work became a public event with church bells pealing, flags fluttering, bands playing and streams of famous visitors, including the Duke of Wellington and Sir Robert Peel.

The ceremonial was an early manifestation of the Brunel touch. Father and son not only liked to do things in style; they created a style

Bridge Street, Blackfriars, where Marc Isambard moved his family in 1824 to be nearer the worksite for the Thames Tunnel. With typical patience and devotion Sophia transformed their house, in what was then an unfashionable neighbourhood, into a stylish and comfortable refuge.

Tunnel works in progress – an idealized view from a German lithograph. Far right, workmen brick up the perilous unsupported gap created between each advance of the shield and the previously completed arch. Above the entrance shaft, left, the pump for removing water and lifting out the excavated earth.

of their own. They had a flair for publicity. It became second nature. It was not enough to invent a machine or design a scheme; the creator had to go out and convince others that it was viable, and to promote public interest and response.

The Thames Tunnel, the first beneath a navigable river, was twelve hundred feet long and took eighteen years and twenty-three days to build. Between 1825 and 1843 it was the scene of fearful hazards and adventures, and there were many casualties. Yet even when disaster threatened, or work had to cease altogether through lack of money, famous men and women from all walks of life and many nations were given V.I.P. treatment at the workings. The public in their thousands paid to participate in one of the wonders of the age – to walk, even for a short distance, beneath the waters of the Thames. This string of visitors provided a small income to the impoverished promoters, even during the seven years when the unfinished tunnel was closed. *The Times* of course christened it 'The Great Bore'. It was the younger Brunel who carried the burden of the work and risked his life – and the lives of others – in hair-raising adventures below ground. Indeed, he grew up with the Tunnel.

There were many references to him in the father's journal. In 1825 for instance:

Isambard incessantly in the works, most actively employed, shows much intelligence. . . . Isambard was the greatest part of the night in the works. . . . Isambard was in the frames the whole night and day till dinner-hour. . . . Isambard the whole day until 2 at night. . . . Isambard has been every night and day too in the works. I relieved him at 3.

Two years later, when some three hundred feet of the Tunnel had been completed, young Isambard celebrated his twenty-first birthday with a party beneath the river. During that month of April 1827 the Tunnel workings, already internationally famous, were a source of public as well as private entertainment. 'By way of calling public attention to the Tunnel', a concert was held and the acoustics were judged remarkably good. Marc Isambard particularly praised the quality of the clarinet. But with upwards of seven hundred visitors coming in every day he also expressed some anxiety.

'Notwithstanding every prudence on our part, a disaster may still occur. *May it not be when the arch is full of visitors!* It is too awful to think of it. I have done my part by recommending to the directors to shut the tunnel.'

Two days later he noted: 'The water increased very much at 9 o'clock. This is very inquiétant! My apprehensions are not groundless. I apprehend nothing, however, as to the safety of the men, but first the visitors, and next, a total invasion of the river. We must be prepared for the Worst.' Even that degree of anxiety did not prevent him from doing the honours the following day.

'I attended Lady Raffles to the frames, most uneasy all the while as if I had a presentiment. . . .'

That same evening the river broke in while young Isambard, his assistant Gravatt and a hundred and sixty men were at the workings. Everybody got out though young Isambard had to go back to rescue others.

Rescue operations after one of the periodic inundations of the tunnel. Though on occasion the water rose almost to the full height of the arches, the greatest danger to workmen lay not in flooding but in the constant threat of disease and blindness from the daily influx of the sewage-filled river.

A diving-bell in use over the site of a breakthrough in the tunnel. After his own descent, IKB wrote of 'the novelty of the thing, the excitement of the occasional risk . . . the crowds of boats to witness our works. . . .'

He wasted no time in attacking the disaster. From the West India Dock Company he borrowed a diving-bell to inspect the hole in the river-bed, and afterwards recorded it all in his journal: 'What a dream it now appears to me! Going down in the diving-bell, finding and examining the hole! The novelty of the thing, the excitement of the occasional risk . . . the crowds of boats to witness our works. . . .'

He also took a boat down inside the workings to inspect the flood within the Tunnel. He made sketches of this hazardous trip and afterwards wrote of it ecstatically:

. . . the hollow rushing of water; the total darkness of all around rendered distinct by the glimmering light of a candle or two, carried by ourselves . . . a dark recess at the end – quite dark – water rushing from it in such quantities as to render it uncertain whether the ground was secure . . . a cavern, *huge*, *misshapen* with water – a cataract coming from it – candles going out. . . .

Incredibly, distinguished sightseers continued to arrive and, pre-sumably as a kind of public relations exercise, young Brunel took them into the flooded workings – even Charles Bonaparte, a non-swimmer, accompanied by the geologist Sir Roderick Murchison who left his own hilarious account of the visit.

The first operation we underwent (one which I never repeated) was to go down in a diving-bell upon the cavity by which the Thames had broken in. Buckland and Featherstonehaugh, having been the first to volunteer, came up with such red faces and such staring eyes, that I felt no great inclination to follow their example, particularly as Charles Bonaparte was most anxious to avoid the dilemma, excusing himself by saying that his family were very short-necked and subject to apoplexy, etc; but it would not do to show the white feather; I got in, and induced him to follow me. The effect was, as I expected, most oppressive, and then on the bottom what did we see but dirty gravel and mud, from which I brought up a fragment of one of Hunt's blacking bottles. We soon pulled the string, and were delighted to breathe the fresh air.

The first folly was, however, quite overpowered by the next. We went down the shaft on the south bank, and got, with young Brunel, into a punt, which he was to steer into the tunnel till we reached the repairing shield. About eleven feet of water were still in the tunnel, leaving just space enough above our heads for Brunel to stand up and claw the ceiling and sides to impel us. As we were proceeding he called out, 'Now, gentlemen, if by accident there should be a rush of water, I shall turn the punt over and prevent you being jammed against the roof, and we shall then be carried out and up the shaft!' On this C. Bonaparte remarked, 'But I cannot swim!' and, just as he had said the words, Brunel, swinging carelessly from right to left, fell overboard, and out went the candles with which he was lighting up the place. Taking this for the *sauve qui peut*, fat C. B., then the very image of Napoleon at St Helena, was about to roll after him, when I held him fast, and, by the glimmering light from the entrance, we found young Brunel, who swam like a fish, coming up on the other side of the punt, and soon got him on board. We of course called out for an immediate retreat, for really there could not be a more foolhardy and ridiculous risk of our lives, inasmuch as it was just the moment of trial as to whether the Thames would make a further inroad or not.

Foolhardiness was to continue. Directors of the Tunnel Company, conducted by young Brunel and an escort of miners, were taking a boat trip to inspect the flooded workings when one of them, a Mr Martin, suddenly stood up in the boat and struck his head on the tunnel roof. He fell backwards against his companions capsizing the boat. Like most of the party Martin was a non-swimmer, and there followed a desperate struggle in the water. In spite of the life-saving efforts of young Isambard one of the miners was drowned.

A workman, lantern in hand, crawls over the huge bank of silt deposited in the tunnel by the first break-through to inspect the shield. Though buried and knocked askew, it remained undamaged by the inundation. Bags of clay, dropped by barge, had stemmed the influx of water, and the tunnel shaft had been partially cleared by pump.

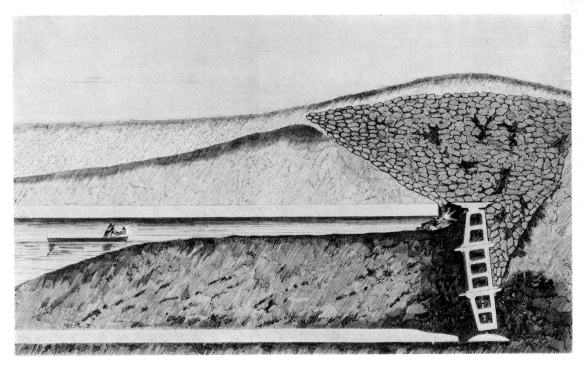

While the Tunnel was being cleared in August 1827 the elder Brunel, harassed by financial worries as the flooding diminished their capital, took to his bed, handing over the superintendence of the work to young Isambard who – at the age of twenty-one – became Resident Engineer.

After a few months of renewed work there was another dramatic exercise in public relations. The sides of the arches were hung with crimson draperies and long tables were laid for dinner – for fifty distinguished guests in one arch and for a hundred and twenty of the workpeople in the adjoining arch. A special feature of the occasion was that the scene was brilliantly lit by great candelabra of a new 'portable gas'. The band of the Coldstream Guards provided musical entertainment. The reason for this extravaganza was to reassure the financial backers and the public in general that the Tunnel was fully restored and that progress was being made.

Toward the middle of January 1828, however, the river broke in again and this time young Brunel himself was a casualty. During his convalescence, he wrote this account of the catastrophe.

I have now been laid up quite useless for 14 weeks and upwards, ever since the 14th January. I shan't forget that day in a hurry, very near finished my journey then; when the danger is over, it is rather amusing than otherwise – while it existed I can't say the feeling was at all uncomfortable. If I was to say the contrary, I should be nearer the truth in this instance. While exertions could still be made and hope remained of stopping the ground it was an excitement which has always been a luxury to me. When we were obliged to run, I felt nothing in particular; I was only thinking of the best way of getting us on and the probable state of the arches. When knocked down, I certainly gave myself up, but I took it very much as a matter of course, which I had expected the moment we quitted the frames, for I never expected we should get out. The instant I disengaged myself and got breath again – all dark – I bolted

Both Brunels combined mechanical genius with the flair of public relations men. In November 1827, to publicize its progress and safety, a great banquet was staged in the tunnel for fifty distinguished guests, with one hundred and twenty miners seated at a separate table. Music was provided by the uniformed band of the Coldstream Guards.

into the other arch – this saved me by laying hold of the railrope – the engine *must* have stopped a minute. I stood still nearly a minute. I was anxious for poor Ball and Collins, who I felt too sure had never risen from the fall we had all had and were, as I thought, *crushed* under the great stage. I kept calling them by name to encourage them and make them also (if still able) come through the opening. While standing there the effect was – *grand* – the roar of the rushing water in a confined passage, and by its velocity rushing past the opening was grand, *very grand*. I cannot compare it to anything, cannon can be nothing to it. At last it came bursting through the opening. I was then obliged to be off – but up to that moment, as far as my sensations were concerned, and distinct from the idea of the loss of six poor fellows whose death I could not then foresee, kept there.

This inundation resulted in seven years of suspended operations during which the Tunnel still remained a spectacle, the workings being sealed off and covered by a great mirror before which the public paid to gaze and wonder.

Young Isambard allowed a touch of facetiousness to temper his despair.

The young Rennies, whatever their real merit, will have built London Bridge, the finest bridge in Europe, and have such a connection with government as to defy competition. Palmer has built new London Docks and thus without labour has established a connection which ensures his fortune, while I – shall have been engaged on the Tunnel which failed, which was abandoned – a pretty recommendation. . . .

I'll turn misanthrope, get a huge Meerschaum, as big as myself and smoke away melancholy – and yet that can't be done without money and that can't be got without working for it. Dear me, what a world this is where starvation itself is an expensive luxury. But damn all croaking, the Tunnel must go on, it shall go on. . . .

He could not of course be expected to live with the Tunnel failure even if it was temporary. He realized that it was necessary in those pioneering, competitive times to build some reputation for himself at once, so he worked at first on a brain child of his father's – a projected 'gaz engine' – obtaining power by generating gas from carbonate of ammonia and sulphuric acid, which was passed over condensers. The experimental plant had been laid down at Rotherhithe on the site of the Tunnel workings, and in April 1829 young Isambard was writing: 'Here I am at Rotherhithe, renewing experiments on gaz – been getting the apparatus up for the last *six months*!! Is it possible? A $\frac{1}{40}$ of the remainder of my life – what a life, the life of a dreamer – am always building castles in the air, what time I waste!' Indeed, it was wasted time. The 'gaz' experiments were abandoned in 1833, when he wrote: 'All the time and expense, both *enormous*, devoted to this thing for nearly 10 years are therefore *wasted*. . . . It must therefore die and with it all my fine hopes – crash – gone – well, well, it can't be helped.'

He was by no means confined to Rotherhithe or to his father's affairs. Without the benefit of railways, he demonstrated unusual mobility, a characteristic of his later life. He was concerned with

A dismantled telescope on the lawn of Sir James South's observatory in Kensington, designed and constructed by IKB during the discouraging period when tunnel work had stopped, the 'gaz' experiments were unsuccessful and his future course remained uncertain.

drainage works at Tollesbury on the Essex coast in 1830 and the following year with the construction of a new dock at Monkwearmouth, Sunderland. Towards the end of that year he covered 528 miles by road sightseeing bridges, cathedrals, docks and at Liverpool took his first journey on the railroad. Two jobs which cropped up in London were disappointing. At Woolwich he made surveys and trial borings for a new dry dock for the Navy Board, who turned him down. At Kensington he worked on the design and construction of an observatory for Sir James South. This was successful enough in itself, being completed in May 1831 with a dinner in celebration at which Brunel in his own words was 'lionized'. But Sir James South declared that the work had exceeded the original estimate and tried to refuse to pay for it. The *Athenaeum*, in an article possibly written by Sir James himself, declared the construction of the observatory to be 'an absurd project' having 'no other object than the display of a *tour de force*, and . . . an effort to produce effect on the part of the architect'. Young Brunel himself was quite capable of dishing out adverse criticism. Asked for his opinion of John Nash's work on the future Buckingham Palace, he declared it to be 'an extraordinary, iniquitous, jobbing, tasteless, unskilful, profligate waste of money. Walls without foundation, ornament without meaning – job, job, job. . . .'

An important ingredient of his character emerges from this period so cluttered with frustration and disappointment – ability to write off loss. He must often have repeated to himself what he wrote about the 'gaz engine'; 'all my fine hopes – crash – gone'. Just as often he must have added to himself 'well, well, it can't be helped'. The acceptance of failure, with a resolve to change course, or to try again, or to do something else, was part of the momentum of his life – and it also contributed to the remarkable vitality and flexibility of his times.

The Tunnel went on with Treasury aid seven years later. In March 1843, by which time young Isambard had fathered Isambard III and was a national figure in his own right, *The Times* reported: 'The ceremony of throwing open this "great bore" to the public was performed on Saturday last under favour of good-natured old Father Thames.' Fifty thousand people paid their pennies to go through within twenty-seven hours of the official opening.

Though Queen Victoria herself walked through it and knighted Marc Isambard, it was only a partial triumph. The horse traffic which was to relieve London's transport never went through. It remained a pedestrian crossing with a sideline of public entertainment, a lurking place not always wholly respectable, until it was taken over by railway interests in the late 1860s; it remains to this day a part of London's Underground Railway system.

The Tunnel injured the younger man but certainly did not blight his life. One important effect of his involvement was noted by his friend and contemporary William Hawes. 'He passed almost direct from boyhood to an equality with any one then in the profession – a position attained by the rapidity and accuracy with which he could apply theory to practice, and support his conclusions by mathematical demonstrations.'

Hawes also recollected:

From 1824 to 1832 he joined his friends in every manly sport; and when, after his accident at the Tunnel, he was obliged to withdraw from more violent exercise, he was still ready to co-operate in the arrangements required to give effect to whatever was in hand. To ensure the success of his friends in a rowing match against time, from London to Oxford and back, in 1828, he designed and superintended the building of a four-oared boat, which, in length and in the proportion of its length to its breadth, far exceeded any boat of the kind which had then been seen on the Thames. . . . The freshness and energy with which he joined in the amusements of his friends after many consecutive days and nights spent in the Tunnel – for frequently he did not go to bed, I might almost say, for weeks together – surprised them all.

The Tunnel accident which for a while put him on his back was a blessing in disguise. It took him out of his father's ambit and stood him on his own – self-critical, ambitious, professionally and mentally alert, physically damaged and materially up against it. Introspection, particularly when he confronted himself in his journals, went with a high-spirited public manner. To the author Charles Macfarlane, who met him on a coach journey during this period, he appeared 'a little, nimble, dark-complexioned man with a vast deal of ready, poignant wit'.

That description held good for most of his working life. He went on as he began, a poet-engineer, exuberant yet disciplined, imaginative

Brighton about 1828, where IKB went to regain his strength after an accident in the tunnel. His recovery hindered by 'returning too soon to a full diet at Brighton', he spent a long convalescence in bed at his father's home on Bridge Street.

The Wapping entrance from a commemorative medal, 1843, upon the opening of the tunnel to pedestrian traffic. Before long the tunnel was to become little more than a side-show and a night-time shelter for the homeless.

yet practical, a humanitarian who could be ruthless with people and never suffered fools gladly. He may have been full of contradictions yet he was a wonderfully integrated man of his time, at once capable of enjoying dazzling successes and of acknowledging devastating failures. Hawes had noticed early his capacity for working without sleep, ignoring all physical discomfort; this obsessional attitude to work drove him on, and ultimately destroyed him. Yet he was born and brought up in relatively comfortable circumstances and did not forego good company, the pleasures of life and of the arts. He loved music, he sketched and painted well. Wryly he confessed to being a great dreamer, building what he called his *châteaux d'Espagne*; yet if ever there was a man of action who made his mark on his century it was I. K. Brunel.

The aftermath of the Tunnel accident was a convalescent period of enforced leisure and no doubt introspection about the Rennies, the Stephensons with their railroads, Telford building his Menai Bridge. Such thoughts did not too much inhibit the young man's appetite for pleasure. His convalescence began at Brighton. 'I met some pleasant company – strolled on the pier smoking my Meerschaum before breakfast; breakfast at twelve. Rode about – went to a Fancy Ball, etc. etc.' A result perhaps of the 'etceteras' was that he had a relapse, returned home 'in a hired chariot' and was put back to bed. 'Mr Travers came and ordered cupping – Mr Travers bled me and prescribed. Feel much better', he wrote hopefully.

The life of Regency Brighton was considered too robust for his further convalescence. So he was sent to Clifton, the suburb of Bristol favoured by its wealthier merchants, where there were few temptations,

THE THAMES TUNNEL.

Fig. 1.

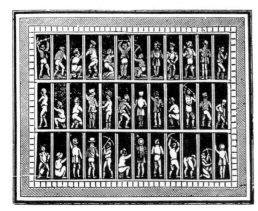

Tunnel construction was often plagued by sightseers, encouraged to visit by curiosity, wonder, and such handbills as this, distributed by the Tunnel Company. (*Left*) A schematic representation of the shield in operation, with workmen occupying all thirty-six compartments.

(*Below*) Debarking from a royal barge, Queen Victoria arrives at Wapping to inspect the newly opened Thames Tunnel in 1843. The Queen demonstrated her interest in the projects of the Brunels on several occasions: in 1842 she had honoured the G.W.R. when she travelled on it, for her first ride by train, from Slough to Paddington.

A view of Bristol and the Avon Gorge before construction began on the Clifton Bridge which now spans the river from a point below the observatory on the far cliff.

at least of a social nature. Here Nature itself provided an allure which was to alter the course of his life. The Avon Gorge, with the tidal river below carrying all the traffic into the port of Bristol, fascinated him. First he sketched it all, then he heard the story of Alderman William Vick who, in 1753, had left money for the building of a bridge across the Gorge. With rising excitement, he learned that there were plans in the air for broaching the legacy and building a bridge.

Thus by great good luck his attention became focused on the building of a bridge in the West of England, for it was in that territory that his railroad ambitions were destined to be magnificently fulfilled. Bristol needed the Avon Bridge. Soon it would be needing a railway.

The Avon Bridge had become a live issue because Vick's bequest to the Society of Merchant Venturers had directed that the money should be allowed to accumulate at compound interest until it reached £10,000, which the good Alderman had regarded as ample to bridge the Gorge. When, in 1829, the sum reached £8,000 a committee had been formed by the Merchant Venturers to consider the best means of carrying out the bequest, raising the balance by subscription.

Vick had specified that the bridge was to be stone-built, but during the years only one individual had come forward with plans to fulfil this requirement. In 1765 William Bridges had produced a rare fantasy. He proposed to fill the whole Gorge with buildings, leaving an immense arch of stone 220 feet high with a 180 foot span for shipping to pass through. A roadway above was to be 50 feet wide and 700 feet long. In the abutments he proposed a vertical township, which included twenty dwelling-houses, a corn exchange, a general market, a water-mill, cotton and wool manufactories, a marine school, a library, a museum, a chapel, coal and stone wharves, a lighthouse, a toll-house, stables, clock-turret and belfry. Mr Bridges was not openly derided, though, not surprisingly, nothing more was heard of him or his plans.

In 1829 it was soon realized that any stone bridge would cost at least £90,000. So in May 1830 the Merchant Venturers went ahead with a Bill to substitute iron for stone and to construct a toll-bridge. Land was purchased in Leigh Woods on the Somerset side and a competition was opened for designs for a suspension bridge. Brunel spent two days making a minute examination of Thomas Telford's four-year-old Menai Suspension Bridge, begun in 1819 and finished in 1826. He benefited from his father's experience on the Ile-de-Bourbon suspension bridges. He then made exquisite sepia drawings and submitted four alternative designs. Their spans lay between 870 and just over 900 feet – all exceeding any suspension bridge then existing. His favourite, nicknamed 'the Grant's Hole' because it was to be sited near the cave of that name, demanded the longest span of all, with a tunnel approach at one end and an arched defile at the other.

There were twenty-two competitors and of these four were selected as possible, one of them Brunel's. The committee, daunted by the imaginative proposals set before them, brought Thomas Telford to adjudicate. Perhaps on account of his advancing years, Telford was

(*Above*) Thomas Telford (1757–1834), son of a Dumfries shepherd, became one of the giants of nineteenth-century engineering. He built roads, docks, canals and bridges, and served as first President of the Institution of Civil Engineers, founded in 1818.

(*Below*) The first, and in many ways most startling, proposal for a bridge over the Avon was that made in 1765 by William Bridges. It called for a vast structure of masonry, almost a city in itself, filling the gorge and permitting river passage through a central arch.

W BRIDGES. *Inven.t et Delin.t* P.D. BRISTOL. *Jan.y* 1793.

Telford's pioneering Menai Bridge, the first major suspension bridge in the world, was part of a new road network he built on government commission to provide rapid access to Ireland from ports in northern Wales.

not at his best. He turned down all the designs, criticizing Brunel's because his proposed spans were too great, stating that six hundred feet, which was the span of his own Menai Bridge, was the limit of safety.

Celia Noble describes the disappointed Brunel as having 'smoked away his anger' – he was already a chain smoker of cigars. Worse was to come. The committee invited Telford himself to submit a design and the master produced a veritable monstrosity, a three-span suspension bridge resting upon two enormous piers rising from the floor of the Gorge, the design including florid Gothic towers and belfries and fretwork over the suspension chains. Incredibly this folly was received with acclamation and engraved, so that thousands of copies could be sold to the public. Brunel, in a letter to the Bridge Committee, made no attack on Telford's style but merely stated that 'As the distance between the opposite rocks was considerably less than what had always been considered as within the limits to which Suspension Bridges might be carried, the idea of going to the bottom of such a valley for the purpose of raising at a great expense two intermediate supporters hardly occurred to me.' Very soon the Committee came to

their senses and changed their minds about the Telford designs, not on the grounds of taste but, face-savingly, 'on account of the inadequacy of the funds requisite for meeting the cost of such high and massive towers as were essential to the plan which that distinguished individual had proposed'.

A new competition was organized in October 1830 with Thomas Telford, this time a competitor, not even short-listed. He had not modified his design and it was rejected. The new referee appointed by the Bridge Trustees was a former President of the Royal Society, a curiously versatile character, Davies Gilbert (1767–1839) M.P. for Bodmin, who had been born Giddy and under that name had been a close friend and correspondent of the Cornish giant Richard Trevithick. Apart from selecting Brunel's design for Clifton Bridge, for which he is duly credited in the *Dictionary of National Biography*, his lasting claim to fame was his editing of the first modern collection of traditional carols. (His two publications in 1822 and 1823 rescued our most cherished Christmas carols from oblivion and added prodigiously to the invention of the nineteenth-century Christmas.) Before tackling the Clifton project Gilbert was modest enough to

Having, as judge, dismissed all the original entries in the Avon bridge competition, Telford was asked to submit his own proposal – and offered this design of astonishing timidity, illogic and lack of grace.

Davies Gilbert, past President of the Royal Society, who judged the second competition. IKB's eloquence and assurance having overcome his initial reservations, Gilbert awarded Brunel the prize, and earned himself the gratitude of posterity for his foresight.

insist on the appointment of a professional engineer as co-referee. He was then joined by John Seaward, a marine-engine builder from the Canal Ironworks, Millwall, whose qualifications to judge bridge design were, to say the least, obscure. Brunel regarded the two of them with a measure of hilarity, writing in his diary 'D. Gilbert came down with *Seaward* to assist him!!!!!!! Seaward!!!!! . . . It appears that my details are found *very bad*, quite inadmissable.'

Out of twelve competitors, Brunel was at first placed second among those short-listed, who were W. Hawks, J. M. Rendel and Captain S. Brown. James Rendel (1799–1856) had worked as a surveyor under Telford and was an experienced constructor of harbours, canals and docks. Samuel Brown (1776–1852), a naval man, later knighted, was known for his work on chain links and was a not always successful pioneer of suspension construction. He had constructed the Old Chain Pier at Leith in 1821; subsequently his best-known work was the ill-fated Chain Pier at Brighton. Hawks was placed first by the referees and was specially commended for the excellence of his detail, but his design was considered to be lacking in strength. Both Rendel and Brown had proposed a span of 780 feet and were turned down, for they failed to meet the stipulation that the load on the suspension chains should not exceed $5\frac{1}{2}$ tons to the square inch. Brunel had sub-mitted a modification of his Grant's Hole design, now offering a massive abutment at Leigh Woods which reduced the span to 630 feet. Squat towers straddling the roadway were to be in the monu-mental style of ancient Egypt. This involved not only sphinxes atop, but the encasement of the towers in metal embossed with scenes showing the work of constructors and illustrating the trades employed in the building and in the manufacture of the material – and required an additional outlay of some £10,000. Though the referees did not turn him down, they raised several serious objections. Further com-promise – and persuasion – were possible. Brunel was on the spot when the result was announced and he at once offered to meet the Bridge Committee and the referees. He succeeded in captivating them with his personality and with what he called his 'Egyptian thing'. He wrote gleefully to his brother-in-law Benjamin Hawes:

. . . of all the wonderful feats I have performed since I have been in this part of the world, I think yesterday I performed the most wonderful. I produced unanimity among fifteen men who were all quarrelling about the most ticklish subject – taste.

The Egyptian thing I brought down was quite extravagantly admired by all and unanimously adopted; and I am directed to make such drawings, lithographs, etc. as I, in my supreme judgment, may deem fit; indeed, they were not only very liberal with their money, but inclined to save themselves much trouble by placing very complete reliance on me.

First estimates of the costs were over £40,000, four times the amount proposed by Alderman Vick, and soon found inadequate. The

One of the three designs in the 'Gothic' style submitted by IKB to the first competition. He carefully explained in his accompanying note that the towers incorporated features drawn from Lancaster Castle and the gateway of Christ Church, Oxford.

Brunel's winning entry in the second competition called for squat suspension towers and anchorages in the Egyptian monumental style. Though, as he wrote, 'The Egyptian thing . . . was quite extravagantly admired by all and unanimously adopted', this part of his design was an early sacrifice to the need for economy.

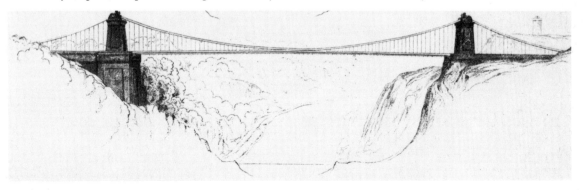

Crossing the Avon Gorge by bar and basket – an entertainment for the bold and a source of petty cash to the enterprising Bridge Trustees during the long period when further construction was suspended.

Egyptian décor was an early sacrifice. The younger Brunel's first great enterprise showed early signs of a chronic family disability – lack of funds. This did not prevent a great junketing when work began in June 1831. Cannon were discharged in the Gorge, the band of the Dragoon Guards played and Sir Abraham Elton pointed a finger of oratory at Brunel with these words: 'The time will come when, as that gentleman walks along the streets or as he passes from city to city, the cry would be raised, "There goes the man who reared that stupendous work, the ornament of Bristol and the wonder of the age."'

This was too optimistic. People's heads were certainly to turn as Isambard Kingdom Brunel passed by: but the Clifton Suspension Bridge was completed only after his death. It was finished in 1864 by a committee of his friends and fellow engineers who stated that they 'had an interest in the work as completing a monument to their late friend Brunel, and at the same time removing a slur from the engineering talent of the country'.

The final work, incorporating chains from Brunel's Hungerford Bridge at Charing Cross, to be mentioned later, differed slightly from his own working designs. The height (road-level above water) was raised from 230 to 245 feet, the chains increased from two to three, and the girders were all iron instead of a combination of wood and iron. The total span (centre to centre of piers) is just over 702 feet. Such deviations have not invalidated the original maintenance tools devised by Brunel. Some of these are still being used.

(*Opposite*) The bridge he called 'my first child, my darling' was to be completed only after Brunel's death. But already in 1831 interest in the project ran so high that artists, painting the scenic Avon Gorge, superimposed the completed bridge upon it.

(*Above*) A panoramic painting of the Avon Gorge during the foundation-laying ceremony for the Leigh Woods abutment in 1836.

(*Left*) The Clifton bridge piers were the only part of his grand design that Brunel was able to see completed.

(*Above*) The Clifton Suspension Bridge as it looks today, utilizing three tiers of chains originally employed in Brunel's Hungerford suspension bridge at Charing Cross.

(*Opposite*) In October 1831, during the nation-wide unrest prior to the passage of the Reform Bill, Bristol was for three days torn by riot and destruction. A bloody cavalry charge in the early morning hours of 31 October brought an end to mob rule in the city.

The very Dragoons whose band had played at the inauguration of works on the bridge were, within a few months, confronting the riotous populace of Bristol. In the autumn of that year, following the rejection of the Reform Bill by the House of Lords, prolonged and bloody riots broke out in Bristol, and the bridge project was driven from men's minds never to revive sufficiently for Brunel to complete the job. After the passage of the Reform Bill in the following year, Brunel occupied himself for the first and last time with active politics. On his own confession it was to compensate for a sorry hiatus in his own affairs. 'I'm unhappy – exceedingly so – the excitement of this election came just in time to conceal it', he wrote to his brother-in-law Benjamin Hawes, who was standing for Lambeth in the Radical cause in the first Reformed Parliament.

Hawes got in and Brunel shone as an electioneer. Subsequently he refused several invitations to stand for Parliament, though fellow engineers such as Robert Stephenson, Joseph Paxton and Joseph Locke went to the House.

Benjamin Hawes, IKB's brother-in-law and admired
friend, eventually became Permanent Under-Secretary of
War and the arch-enemy of Florence Nightingale.

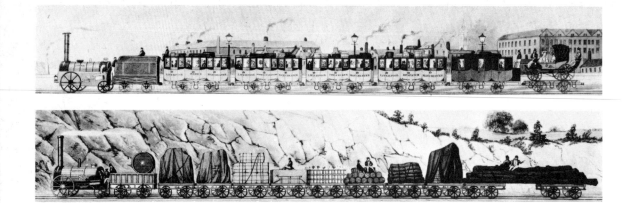

Carriages in use in 1834 on the Liverpool & Manchester Railway, the world's first fully scheduled service for passengers and goods. The growing threat of Liverpool to the port of Bristol gave impetus to the construction of the G.W.R.

With Ben Hawes returned and the Clifton Bridge held up through lack of funds, Brunel's despondency was relieved by another project which cropped up and, fortunately, kept him in Bristol. The City was uneasy that its position as Britain's greatest port outside London was being threatened by Liverpool, where enclosed wet-docks had been built. Brunel had been called upon to propose improvements to the harbour facilities at Bristol. Because of the riots his suggestions had been pigeon-holed, but after the election he was given the job of implementing them.

While this work progressed rapidly and well, activity at Clifton started again slowly. The laying of the foundation-stone of the Leigh Woods abutment did not take place until 1836. Then, a year later, there was a further hold-up when the contractors went bankrupt. The only crossing of the Gorge meanwhile was by means of an iron bar one thousand feet long and one and a half inches in diameter from which a basket was suspended. It ran downhill by gravitation and was hauled up by ropes. Soon after this vertiginous contraption was erected an unauthorized user got stuck in the middle, owing to a bend in the bar, and narrowly escaped with his life. His crossing had been made without Brunel's permission and there was a great to-do about it. A new bar having been fixed, Brunel himself, accompanied by a lad, made the first passage across to make sure that the thing was safe for others. The basket and bar ironically turned out to be the only profitable aspect of the enterprise. When work ground to a halt in May 1854 with only two piers standing, the bar and basket remained as a public entertainment and a source of revenue. The Bridge Trustees charged at first five shillings, later reduced to a shilling a head, for the foolhardy to cross, and in twelve months made £125.

Another good reason for the citizens of Bristol to cast a wary eye towards Liverpool was the opening in 1830 of George Stephenson's Liverpool & Manchester Railway, the second in the country and soon to continue a line of communication with the metropolis. As early as 1824, some Bristol merchants had formed 'The London and Bristol Rail-Road Co.' whose directors included John London Macadam of road fame. Their idea had been to run a railway and turnpike road together, the road 'passing through the towns instead of near them as the Railroad must necessarily do'. This came to nothing as did two or three more schemes. It was not until 1832 that a lively and influential committee of four wealthy men, representing Bristol Corporation, the Dock Company, the Chamber of Commerce and the Society of Merchant Venturers, agreed on the provision of funds for a preliminary survey and estimate, and advertised for an engineer to carry this out.

Brunel was on the spot and his mind was on railways. As Engineer for the Avon Bridge and the harbour works, he was a favourite candidate for the survey. There were other candidates, however, with local associations, and the contest looked like being a close one. When some members of the Committee announced that they would take the man who put in the lowest estimate for making the survey, Brunel showed his mettle. 'You are holding out', he wrote to the Committee, 'a premium to the man who will make you the most flattering promises. It is quite obvious that the man who has either least reputation at stake, or who has most to gain by temporary success, and least to lose by the consequences of disappointment, must be the winner in such a race.'

This show of integrity won him the job. When he was appointed in March 1833, the situation was summarized by Hamilton Ellis: 'Having persuaded the Railway Committee to run him, I. K. Brunel was on his way to running the Railway Committee and moulding the form of the railway company to be.' The Great Western Railway, the second great trunk-railway out of London, was very much the creation of the poet-engineer, the practical dreamer.

From March until May 1833 he added horsemanship to his accomplishments in a veritable assault-course between Bristol and London. Almost every day and all day in the saddle, at night he was engrossed in the paper work of the preliminary survey to establish the line of the G.W.R., which with little modification was to become reality. 'Between ourselves,' he wrote, 'it is harder work than I like. I am rarely under twenty hours a day at it.'

As assistants he appointed W. H. Townsend and later a surveyor named Hughes. Both men had a foretaste of the formidable energy and personal demands which soon earned the young Brunel the nickname 'Little Giant.' Brunel's diary for the period reflects in terse terms some of the rigours they shared. On the very first day for instance: 'Started with Townsend (who as usual was late). Went up the B & G line and then across the country by Wick Court and over the hill into Lanbridge Valley and into the London Road by Bath. A most circuitous line and dreadfully hilly country, but I fear the only line

The locomotives built by George Stephenson (1781–1848) and his son Robert were adopted for use in Europe and Canada as well as in England. His celebrated *Rocket* won a competition for the Liverpool & Manchester Railway in 1829.

which will take in the present railway. Dined at Bath and rode home by the lower road. This latter line, I think, offers greater facilities.'

That poor Hughes may have had some difficulty in keeping up with the pace is suggested by several entries during that April.

Thurs. April 18th – Got a hack and rode out to Wo. Hill according to the letter from Hughes. After some search found him – on the wrong track. Directed him as he was so far to push on to the Thames across Early Court and Upper Early and the next morning to begin again at Chapple Green and go on to Shinfield Green where I would meet him on Saturday morning.

I then rode on to Bagshot Heath and returned by a line going at the back of East-hampstead Park. My horse came down at Mitchell.

Sat. April 20th. – Arrived at Reading late. Went to bed. After breakfast went in search of Hughes. After some trouble found him at 'Black Boy', Shinfield, gave him maps. With him to Theal Road and into Pangbourne. Returned to Reading, went to Theale. Met a Mr Keeps who shewed me the new church. Returned to Reading; Hughes came in the evening. Gave him £5. 0. 0.

Monday April 22nd. – Started at 6 a.m. Examined the ground in the neighbourhood of Wantage – breakfasted at Streatley. Determined on the outer line winding round the undulating ground. Returned to Reading, dined, and went to Theal to meet Hughes. After waiting some time gave it up and returned.

Tuesday April 23rd. – After breakfast went in search of Hughes; after some trouble found him at the canal between Shinfield and Calcott Mills, a beautiful place this in hot weather. Gave him the line to Wantage.

Just before his survey was completed in May, he managed to live through what must have been an exceptional Monday even for him:

Monday May 6th. – Started by Emerald Coach to Newbury. Arrived there, mounted my horse and rode to Uffington, thence to Shrivenham. Slept there and in the morning proceeded to Swindon. Met Hughes there – found letters from Osborne requiring my immediate return to town. George [?] came; our lines nearly meet, but he has been winding round in a most curious manner. Directed him to point his Bench Mark to Hughes at Wootton Bassett and then return over his ground to Chippenham following a line I traced for him. Rode to Hungerford; thence to Newbury. Just as I got in sight of the Castle my horse came down – cut his knees and forehead dreadfully – just scratched my knee. I never saw a horse tumble over in such an '*abandonné*' style, he dirtied himself even over the withers and croup he rolled over so far. Bled him and left him at the Castle. Returned to town in Bristol Mail.

This preliminary survey, completed punctually for the Committee in May 1833, recommended a route from Bristol through Chippenham and the Vale of the White Horse, striking the Thames near Cholsey, thence to Reading and Maidenhead with alternative routes on to London. The most controversial aspect of this was the proposal for a tunnel over three thousand yards long, through the oolite ridge near

(*Opposite*) IKB in his thirties, from a painting by John Horsley. His hand rests on a map of the route he surveyed for the G.W.R.

Box on the Chippenham–Bath section. Foremost among those who denounced this was Richard Cort, an industrialist, who should have known better, but who had a strong bias against steam on roads.

Though the G.W.R. probably may reach as far as Bath from Bristol, after having, like a mole, explored its way through tunnels long and deep, the shareholders who travel by it will be so heartily sick, what with foul air, smoke, and sulphur, that the very mention of a railway will be worse than Ipecacuanha, especially when the only prospect they can find in the least cheering in the middle of all the derangement of their stomachs will be a granite tramway actually in operation alongside of their own dose of Ipecacuanha, ready to follow up the black draft, so as to get rid of every particle of obstruction with which the bottom of their pockets may otherwise be afflicted. . . .

He did not hesitate to rake up the earlier Brunel failure, referring to 'the gratification of Mr Brunel, who may wish to tunnel more successfully for the Great Western Bubble through dry land than has hitherto rewarded the ingenuity and talent of his father through wet land'.

Nevertheless the preliminary report, with Brunel's first estimate of the cost of the line at just over £2,800,000, enabled his Bristol Committee to hold a public meeting. 'Got through it very tolerably', wrote Brunel, who then assisted at the creation of a London Committee whom he described as 'rather an old woman's set'. He was now rearing to go. There was a detailed survey to do. Capital of £3,000,000 was needed, half to be subscribed before the Bill for the railway could be presented to Parliament.

Nowhere is Brunel's eye better demonstrated than in the magnificent proportions, the combination of massiveness and grace, that mark his work along the path of the G.W.R. This triumphal portal of the Box Tunnel proclaims his architectural, as well as his engineering, skill.

After intense debate in Parliament and prolonged public opposition, the G.W.R. company was at last incorporated in 1835 and took up offices in this building in the Strand.

Brunel and his colleagues were dealing mainly with people who had never seen a railway. There was massive distrust. Had not the Iron Duke himself gone on record with the misgiving that the new railroads 'would encourage the lower classes to move about'? Landowners viewed them sometimes with outrage, as a threat to amenities or property values, and sometimes just with avarice. Exorbitant sums were demanded and outrageous conditions imposed – for example, the Squire of Kemple insisted upon a quarter of a mile of the line being hidden by a tunnel. Because this hundred and twenty miles of line to the West encountered exceptionally powerful landowning and vested interests, not to mention institutional obstacles such as those of Eton College, the passage of its Bill through Parliament was uniquely strenuous and prolonged, costing the Company nearly £90,000 in legal and Parliamentary expenses.

In a letter written years later to Brunel's son, St George Burke, Q.C., recollected:

In 1833 your father and I occupied chambers facing each other in Parliament Street, and as my duties involved the superintendence, as Parliamentary agent, of the compliance with all the Standing Orders of Parliament, and very frequent interviews and negotiations with the landowners on the line, we were of necessity constantly thrown together. To facilitate our intercourse, it occurred to your father to carry a string across Parliament Street, from his chambers to mine, to be there connected with a bell, by which he could either call me to the window to receive his telegraphic signals, or, more frequently, to wake me up in the morning when we had occasion to go into the country together, which, it is needless to observe, was of frequent occurrence; and great was the astonishment of the neighbours at this device, the object of which they were unable to comprehend.

I believe that at that time he scarcely ever went to bed, though I never remember to have seen him tired or out of spirits. He was a very constant smoker, and would take his nap in an arm-chair, very frequently with a cigar in his mouth; and if we were to start out of town at five or six o'clock in the morning, it was his frequent practice to rouse me out of bed about three, by means of the bell, when I would invariably find him up and dressed, and in great glee at the fun of having curtailed my slumbers by two or three hours more than necessary.

No one would have supposed that during the night he had been poring over plans and estimates, and engrossed in serious labours, which to most men would have proved destructive of their energies during the following day; but I never saw him otherwise than full of gaiety, and apparently as ready for work as though he had been sleeping through the night.

In those days we had not the advantage of railways, and were obliged to adopt the slower, though perhaps not less agreeable, mode of travelling with post-horses. Your father had a britzska, so arranged as to carry his plans and engineering instruments, besides some creature comforts, never forgetting the inevitable cigar-case among them; and we would start by daybreak, or sometimes earlier, on our country excursions, which still live in my remembrance as some of the pleasantest I have ever enjoyed; though I think I may safely say that, pleasurable as they were, we never lost sight of the business in which we were engaged. . . .

We canvassed many landowners together, and I had plenty of opportunities of judging of his skill and caution in our discussions with them, though we had many a good laugh afterwards. . . .

At Westminster Brunel shone. The Bill was at first rejected by the Lords after fifty-seven hours in Commons committee. At a second attempt it was forty days in a committee of the Lords. The burden of much of this rested on Brunel. During the Commons committee he endured for eleven days what was afterwards described as 'so protracted a cross-examination [as] has probably never been heard in any court or committee-room'. From such endurance tests he emerged in his thirtieth year with his reputation as an engineer immensely and deservedly enhanced.

The committee-room [wrote an eyewitness] was crowded with landowners and others interested in the success or defeat of the Bill, and eager to hear Brunel's evidence. His knowledge of the country surveyed by him was marvellously great, and the explanations he gave of his plans, and the answers he returned to questions suggested by Dr Lardner, showed a profound acquaintance with the principles of mechanics. He was rapid in thought, clear in his language, and never said too much, or lost his presence of mind. I do not remember ever having enjoyed so great an intellectual treat as that of listening to Brunel's examination, and I was told at the time that George Stephenson and many others were much struck by the ability and knowledge shown by him.

George Stephenson, who, with such engineers as Joseph Locke and Charles Vignoles, was supporting the project, said in his evidence: 'I can imagine a better line, but I do not know of one so good.' The doctor mentioned in the report was Dr Dionysius Lardner (1793–1859), an egregious pseudo-scientific know-all who, besides being a prolific author, blinded large audiences in Britain and America with a bizarre mixture of knowledge and nonsense, comic enough in hindsight but a tiresome force to be reckoned with at the time. Objecting to Brunel's proposal for the G.W.R. to pass through the Box Tunnel with a gradient of one in one hundred – admittedly the most controversial of the plans – Lardner sought to prove that a train entering such a tunnel and having brake failure would emerge at the other end doing a hundred and twenty miles an hour, the passengers being 'unable to breathe'. Suffering fools was not I. K. Brunel's strongest point; nevertheless, he patiently explained that the Doctor had overlooked such factors as friction and air resistance and that the speed of the supposed runaway train could not exceed fifty-six miles an hour.

Such factual defeats did not diminish the stature of the batty Doctor whose publications included works on the habits of white ants and the uranography of Saturn, and whose private reputation was somewhat dented by his eloping with a Mrs Mary Heaviside. He was to return to assault Brunel on several future occasions. The tunnel was the target for many other objections.

One witness declared that it was 'monstrous, extraordinary, most dangerous, and impracticable' and that it would 'cause the wholesale destruction of human life'. Another said that 'no person would desire to be shut out from the daylight with a consciousness that he had a superincumbent weight of earth sufficient to crush him in case of accident'.

Other objections suggested that the opening of the railway would choke the Thames for want of traffic, destroy the drainage of the Thames Valley and leave Windsor Castle unsupplied with water. It was said that Eton College would be ruined because London would pour forth 'the most abandoned of its inhabitants to come down by the railway and pollute the minds of the scholars, whilst the boys themselves would take advantage of the short interval of their play hours to run up to town, mix in all the dissipation of London life, and return before their absence could be discovered'. The formidable Dr Edward Hawtrey, the Headmaster, felt sure that railways would destroy the classical tradition – and worse, schoolmasters would be superseded by *mistresses*. He declared that Homer, Virgil, Horace (but not Ovid's *Art of Love*) would be thrust aside in favour of the dangerous thoughts of Rousseau and Voltaire. He was good at his own job, doubling the number of pupils during his reign. That he was a man of influence was proved when the Company was prevented from building a station within three miles of the College. The station at Slough, and later the branch line to Windsor, materialized only after royal pressure.

From London the most powerful objections arose out of Brunel's brilliant notion to terminate the line at Vauxhall; he was alone in seeing the advantages of a future link across the Thames with railways which would provide a through service to the Continent. This would have meant that the line would go from Ealing through Brompton, described by counsel as 'the most famous of any place in the neighbourhood of London for the salubrity of its air'. Here and in Chelsea it was suggested that 'streams of fire would proceed from the locomotive engines' and destroy the amenities. The landowners of that part of London kept the line at bay. Even the suggestion of a terminus behind the Hoop and Toy public house at South Kensington was turned down, and the less socially inviolate Paddington Green was finally selected for the London station.

Public protest in London was centred in the fear of loss in property values along the proposed path of the line to its terminus.

(*Below, right*) The Reverend Edward Hawtrey, Headmaster of Eton, feared the disruptive effects of the railway upon the lives of his students. His opposition kept the G.W.R. from placing a station within three miles of the school.

PROPOSED GREAT
WESTERN RAILWAY.
NOTICE
TO

Landowners, Householders, and Occupiers of Lands and Tenements, in the Line of Road proposed to be taken by the Great Western Railroad.

A BILL having been brought into Parliament to erect a Viaduct for the purpose of the Great Western Railroad from Vauxhall Bridge, through parts of the PARISHES of ST. GEORGE, HANOVER-SQUARE, CHELSEA, BROMPTON, and KENSINGTON, the Parties interested in this Line are requested to attend

A PUBLIC MEETING
TO BE HELD AT THE

BELGRAVE HOTEL, Ebury-street, Pimlico,
On Wednesday next, March 5th, at 11 o'Clock.

The Right Hon. the EARL CADOGAN
Will take the Chair at 12 o'Clock, precisely.

This proposed Viaduct is to be ERECTED on BRICK or STONE ARCHES, from TWENTY-FIVE to THIRTY FEET high, by which the many Houses in the Line and in the Neighbourhood will be deprived of Light and the Free Circulation of Air, and be exposed to a most incessant and frightful Noise, much aggravated by the reverberation of the Arches, from the ENGINES, and LONG TRAINS OF HEAVY CARRIAGES TRAVELLING at a height equal to the level of the Second Floor Windows. The immense deterioration in the value of all Property near which this Viaduct will pass, for which no adequate Remuneration can be given, requires the immediate and particular attention of every Person interested in Property in these Parishes, to oppose such Parts of the Bill as may affect their several Interests.

The Sonning cutting in progress. Many almost insuperable difficulties were encountered in easing gradients, constructing viaducts and boring the nearly two-mile-long Box Tunnel, and Brunel himself was often forced to take personal command.

Immediately the Act was through in September 1835, work started simultaneously at the London and the Bristol ends of the line. From London, Brunel sent instructions for his Bristol men to get the thick underwood in Birslington cut, so that he could immediately determine the course of the line when he went down the following week. 'We shall have our flags flying over the Brent Valley tomorrow. I should not wish that Bristol should fancy itself left behind.' Thus he set the pace which even by this century's motorway standards was remarkable. In just over five and a half years the first train would be running between the two cities.

On Boxing Night 1835, some four months after the start of the work, Brunel, sitting alone and late by his fireside in his Parliament Street office, took down his long-neglected diary:

When I last wrote in this book I was just emerging from obscurity. I had been toiling most unprofitably at numerous things – unprofitably at least at the moment. The Railway certainly was brightening but still very uncertain – what a change. *The Railway* now is in progress. I am their Engineer to the finest work in England – a handsome salary – £2,000 a year – on excellent terms with my Directors and all going smoothly, but what a fight we have had – and how near defeat – and what a ruinous defeat it would have been. It is like looking back upon a fearful pass – but we have succeeded. And it's not this alone but everything I have been engaged in has been successful.

The office fire kindled a boastful glow in him – an honest, flagrant but justifiable boast as he went over his score.

'*Clifton Bridge* – my first child, my darling, is actually going on –

The enormous increase in trade in the early nineteenth century led to the need for expanded dock facilities in every major port. The commission to construct a new dock at Monkwearmouth (Sunderland) was IKB's first important one of this kind. A short time later he was responsible for improvements in Bristol Harbour as well.

recommenced work last Monday – Glorious!! *Sunderland Docks* too going well – *Bristol* Docks. All Bristol is alive and turned bold and speculative with this Railway – we are to widen the entrances and the Lord knows what.'

He added to his list the pros and cons of the Merthyr & Cardiff Railway, the Cheltenham Railway, and the Bristol & Exeter Railway. He went on somewhat disparagingly about his Hungerford pedestrian bridge at Charing Cross.

Suspension Bridge across Thames – I have condescended to be engineer to this – but I shan't give myself much trouble about it. If done, however, it all adds to my stock of irons.

I think this forms a pretty list of real profitable, sound professional jobs – unsought for on my part, that is given to me fairly by the respective parties, all, except M D [Monkwearmouth Dock] resulting from the Clifton Bridge – which I fought hard for and gained only by persevering struggles and some manœuvres (all fair and honest however). *Voyons*. . . .

A pretty considerable capital likely to pass through my hands – and this at the age of 29 – faith not so young as I always fancy tho' I really can hardly believe it when I think of it.

I am just leaving 53 Parliament St where I may say I have made my fortune or rather the foundation of it and have taken Lord Devon's house, No. 18 Duke Street – a fine house – I have a fine travelling carriage – I go sometimes with my 4 horses – I have a cab & horse, I have a secretary – in fact I am now somebody.

Everything has prospered, everything at this moment is sunshine. I don't like it – it can't last – bad weather must surely come. Let me see the storm in time to gather in my sails.

Mrs B. – I foresee one thing – this time 12 months I shall be a married man. How will that be? Will it make me happier?

In less than twelve months he was a married man. The Mrs B. to set off his success story had materialized in the person of Mary Horsley, gifted with the grand manner, nicknamed 'Duchess of Kensington' by her own family. She did indeed make him happier, in that she was one of his achievements. She fulfilled his need for a home and family life – she bore him three children – and she gave it all style. What was lacking in enduring passion was made up in her cool beauty, her manipulation of wealth and reputation, her drawing-room attracting the famous and cultured, even her pair of silk-upholstered carriages and the footman following her as she strolled in St James's Park. Isambard created it all, and it enhanced his reputation: Mary accepted it all and reigned. The marriage was prosperous and happy enough, though Isambard spelt out the truth in a diary entry: 'My profession is after all my only fit wife. . . .'

The only other woman to whom he became overtly attracted was the very old and grand Lady Holland, the great Whig hostess who reigned at Holland House. When she in her seventies ventured on her first railway journey in 1841 Brunel attended her and held her hand, it was said, the whole way from Paddington to Chippenham. Close friendship developed from this, with frequent notes from the great

Mary Horsley Brunel. Her beauty, elegance and style provided a fitting social milieu for Brunel's growing professional success.

Though hard work made his fame, some of Brunel's charm and playfulness, some of the pleasure he took in life, seems to break through this formal portrait by John Horsley.

lady such as the one inviting him 'any day that may suit you, at seven o'clock to eat your *Soupe. . . .*'

His offices at Duke Street, to which he could retire at any moment, day or night, were on the ground floor. The 'Duchess' ruled upstairs where the stylish decorations included work specially commissioned from Landseer. The Brunels moved in a world where there was a healthy mingling between the arts and science and technology. Mary's family connections brought Isambard abundant opportunity to turn from the drawing-board to the music-room, from the board-room to the easel. Mary's younger sister, for instance, had captured for her album the signatures of Brahms, Chopin, Paganini and Felix Mendelssohn, the last being a frequent visitor to the Horsley home and subsequently to Duke Street. Though Isambard did not play any instrument, he was passionately fond of music and a keen opera-goer. His talents for drawing and painting brought him into close and lasting harmony with Mary's brother, John Horsley, who became a Royal Academician and left the best likenesses of Mary and Isambard. 'He criticized with great keenness and judgment a drawing which I had with me', John Horsley recalled, 'and at the same time gave me a lesson on paper straining. From that time till his death he was my most intimate friend.'

During work on the South Devon Railway Brunel became enchanted by the prospect from the fields at Watcombe, near Torquay. Having purchased the land, he sketched designs for a great house to fulfil his childhood dreams.

(*Left*) Lady Holland (1770–1845), at Holland House. The famous hostess's apprehensions induced Brunel to accompany her on her first railway journey, and this contact ripened into friendship.

(*Above*) IKB often travelled abroad with his brother-in-law and close friend, John Horsley (1817–1903), with whom he shared a love of drawing and painting.

IKB's offices on the ground floor of his home at 18 Duke Street. The family circle often suffered his absence while Brunel devoted himself to his 'only fit wife', his profession.

Mary proved to be a poor traveller – the Alps made her dizzy – and John went on many continental trips with Isambard. A more profound intimacy developed in after years when sorrow and disappointment afflicted both of them, and John Horsley wrote in a letter that was never delivered:

I would implore you to reflect upon that hour of death which must come upon you sooner or later, and whether, at that awful moment, you will be able to look with satisfaction upon your life, which has been one of almost unparalleled devotion to your profession, to the exclusion, to far too great an extent, of that which was due to your God and even to your family, and with an utter disregard of your health. . . .

My dear friend, will all this bring you peace at the last?

Isambard, who had been brought up Protestant, was not as outwardly God-fearing as some of his friends and contemporaries. In all his grandiose schemes he did not leave too much to God, though he commended the value of prayer to his son:

I am not prepared to say that the prayers of individuals can be separately and individually granted, that would seem to be incompatible with the regular movements of the mechanism of the Universe, and it would seem impossible to explain why prayer should now be granted, now refused; but this I can assure you, that I have ever, in my difficulties, prayed fervently, and that – in the end – my prayers have been, or have *appeared* to me to be, granted, and I have received great comfort.

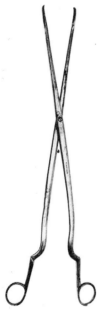

With a recalcitrant half-sovereign stuck in his throat, Brunel remained cool enough to design these forceps, nearly two feet long, for the surgeon Sir Benjamin Brodie to use in attempting a tracheotomy.

This no doubt carefully considered statement was his only religious advice on record. For the rest, he was an ambitious parent, influenced by the practical and wide-ranging guidance he had received from his own father. His eldest son, Isambard III, was a disappointment: he was born partially crippled and showed no aptitude for engineering. He entered the law, became Chancellor of the Diocese of Ely and wrote the first biography of his father, which was published in 1870. The younger son, Henry Marc, entered fully into the parental activities and subsequently became a partner of Sir John Wolfe Barry, assisting him in the design of the Tower Bridge. The daughter, Florence, married Arthur James, the Eton master renowned for his ghost stories.

In spite of the grandeur of the drawing-room and the austerities of work in the office downstairs, there was plenty of fun in Duke Street for the young family. A most popular nursery event was Papa's performance of a coin-swallowing trick. In 1843 when Isambard, at the age of thirty-seven, had become a household name, the nursery relaxation took a sinister turn. He swallowed the coin. It was a half-sovereign, and it lodged in his windpipe, threatening him with choking to death. In the ensuing excitement Brunel kept wonderfully cool. He designed an instrument for the surgeon Sir Benjamin Brodie to use in carrying out a tracheotomy operation. This was unsuccessful, though the instrument is still known as 'Brodie's Forceps'.

The news of the intractable coin spread far and wide. After Brodie's failure, the medical profession was baffled; but Brunel himself was undaunted. He sketched out an apparatus upon which he could be strapped, turned upside-down and swung rapidly, head over heels, in order to make the half-sovereign drop out by centrifugal force. A choking fit spoilt the first attempt, but on the second the coin duly dropped from his mouth. 'I was safely and comfortably delivered of my little coin . . .' he wrote to a friend at Bristol, 'with hardly an effort it dropped out, as many another has, and I hope will, drop out of my fingers. I am perfectly well, and expect to be at Bristol by the end of the week.' His fame was such that Macaulay, hearing of his delivery, ran through the Athenaeum Club crying 'It's out, it's out' and everyone knew what was meant.

The Reverend Richard H. Barham's celebration of the event in *The Ingoldsby Legends* may well have had something of a double edge – for many persisted in regarding Brunel's versatility and enterprise as a bag of tricks.

Charles Alexander Saunders, Secretary to the London Committee of the G.W.R., who quickly became one of Brunel's staunchest friends and supporters. Much of the railway's success was due to his efforts in raising capital and smoothing resistance to its advance.

> *All conjuring's bad! They may get in a scrape*
> *Before they're aware, and, whatever its shape,*
> *They may find it no easy affair to escape.*
> *It's not everybody that comes off so well*
> *From 'leger de main' tricks as Mr Brunel.*

Besides conjuring tricks, Duke Street sometimes offered those more sophisticated entertainments described by Brunel's grand-daughter, Lady Celia Noble:

The rooms lent themselves readily to the private theatricals so much loved by the family, and permitted more ambitious efforts than at High Row. There were 'tableaux' of scenes from Flaxman's *Odyssey*, in which Mary, with her classical features and stately figure, represented Penelope with her suitors, using an elaborate loom made by Webbe, the famous upholsterer of Bond Street; and there were frequent cathedral interiors with appropriate music from Mendelssohn on the organ in the back drawing-room; Isambard, now the important business man, no longer played farcical parts, but in spare moments designed mechanical contrivances for the scenery.

The elegant make-believe upstairs provided a dramatic contrast with the wear and tear of railway-building in the downstairs office. Mary may have chosen acquaintances for their social or artistic qualities; in a different way, Isambard was also discriminating in his personal friends. Some of his most rewarding relationships were with his colleagues. Charles Saunders, the Secretary of the London Committee of the G.W.R. who devoted his whole working life to the line, received this personal note at the end of a long letter from Brunel: 'I have spun this long yarn, partly as a recreation after working all the night, principally to have the pleasure of telling a real friend that I am sensible of his kindness, although he hardly allows me to see it, and partly because I wish you to know that if I appear to take things coldly it is because I am obliged to harden myself a little to be able to bear the thought of it. . . .' On similar terms he could communicate with Christopher Claxton, Thomas Guppy, Daniel Gooch, all colleagues and devoted friends. He enjoyed also singularly warm friendships with fellow and often rival engineers such as Robert Stephenson and Joseph Locke.

He could be benignly exacting towards those who worked for him. To an unlucky employee who was falling short on efficiency he wrote:

Plain, gentlemanly language seems to have no effect upon you. I must try stronger language and stronger measures. You are a cursed, lazy, inattentive, apathetic vagabond, and if you continue to neglect my instructions, and to show such infernal laziness, I shall send you about your business. I have frequently told you, amongst other absurd, untidy habits, that that of making drawings on the back of others was inconvenient; by your cursed neglect of that you have again wasted more of my time than your whole life is worth, in looking for the altered drawings you were to make of the Station – they won't do.

The choice of the right men, and their organization and management, were just as vital as technical know-how. Brunel's contemporaries such as the Stephensons managed work forces on an unprecedented scale, but none equalled Brunel's control in his heyday of very large labour operations in diverse fields simultaneously. He was good at delegating. He was approachable. He demanded and gave loyalty. He inspired his people. There might be liveried footmen at Duke Street, but he could and would throw off his coat and work alongside any man he employed. Short in stature, great in energy, he was widely known as the 'Little Giant'.

He got on famously with navvies and shipyard workers. He was adept at the sort of gesture which became a legend. After a force of four thousand men and three hundred horses had been working day and night from opposite ends on the Box Tunnel, Brunel was on the spot when the two bores met. He was so delighted with the accuracy of the operation that he took a ring from his finger and presented it to the ganger in charge: and the story of this was always cherished long after the casualties were forgotten. In his world casualties were a calculated risk. When he was shown a list of more than a hundred and thirty of the Box navvies admitted to Bath Hospital between September 1839 and June 1841, he stated: 'I think it is a small list considering the very heavy works and the immense amount of powder used. . . .'

Apart from man-management his letter-books reflect the keen eye for human character needed in the business of railway construction.

(*Above, opposite*) Navvies at work hauling earth to establish a firm embankment in the early days of rail construction.

(*Below, opposite*) The creation of decent housing and social facilities for railworkers was a prominent feature in the plans for the new town of Swindon (seen here in an aerial view), chosen as the main locomotive depot and repair shop for the G.W.R.

The Earl of Carnarvon was only one of the many landowners whose interests had to be conciliated in gaining the right of way for the G.W.R. Brunel overcame most objections by tact, charm and, wherever necessary, willing concessions to the humble as well as the great.

Mr Northcote's orchards were 'to be bought by tunnelling only under one corner and paying him well for it'; a clergyman's pond had to be removed 'but he is to have a dozen fish ponds farther from the line for the same money'. A Miss Payne wished the line to be fifty yards away from her fence – 'better not hamper ourselves with any positive engagement with Miss Payne, still, no difficulty in moving line a little farther off, and I have no objection in saying that we will do all in our power to accommodate her'. The influential required special tact. 'If Lord G. Somerset takes part against us, much better make up our minds to concession indeed, as he would be a formidable opponent.' To Paul Methuen M.P. who wanted a deviation from the neighbourhood of Corsham Park: '. . . I know the Directors will be very desirous to consult your wishes as far as they can consistently with their duty. The interests of the Company are much concerned with removal of the personal opposition of a landowner of your influence.' The Earl of Carnarvon was told: 'The Company are anxious that no individual should suffer loss or injury and are prepared to consider and agree upon compensation, also accommodation to be afforded to the tenants by bridges and communications. Under these circumstances, I trust your Lordship will view the measure in the same favourable light as the other Noblemen and Gentlemen, large proprietors, in the same neighbourhood.'

After conciliating the mighty, Brunel revelled in the asides he committed to his diary or wrote in private letters. At a moment when his whole career was threatened, he wrote to his close friend Thomas Guppy, the Bristol sugar merchant and one of the founders of the G.W.R.: 'A splendid storm is brewing and although I have no umbrella or shelter and must weather it out one is curious to know beforehand whether it will be snow, hail or rain or all three – and thunder and lightning to boot. . . . I am by no means disposed to treat it lightly though a good attack always warms my blood and raises my spirits.'

His letters acted as safety-valves for the terrific pressures of his daily life. He loved to let off steam, even to Mary whose gifts did not include a sense of humour.

Wootton Bassett

My DEAREST MARY,

I have become quite a walker. I have walked today from Bathford Bridge to here – all but about one mile, which makes eighteen miles walking along the line – and I really am not very tired. I am, however, going to sleep here – if I had been half an hour earlier, I think I could not have withstood the temptation of coming up by the six $\frac{1}{2}$ train, and returning by the morning goods train, just to see you; however, I will write you a long letter instead. It is a blowy evening, pouring with rain, my last two miles were wet. I arrived of course rather wet, and found the *Hotel*, which is the best of a set of deplorable public houses, full – and here I am at the 'Cow and Candle-

snuffers' or some such sign – a large room or cave, for it seems open to the wind everywhere, old-fashioned, with a large chimney in one corner; but unfortunately it has
one of these horrible little stoves, just nine inches across. I have piled a fire upon both
hobs, but to little use, there are four doors and two windows. What's the use of the
doors I can't conceive, for you might crawl under them if they happened to be
locked, and they seem too crooked to open, the two ones with not a bad looking bit
of glass between, seem particularly friendlily disposed.

The window curtains very wisely are not drawn, as they would be blown right
across the room and probably over the two extra greasy muttons which are on the
table, giving just light enough to see the results of their evident attempt to outvie
each other, trying which can make the biggest snuff. One of them is quite a splendid
fellow, a sort of black colliflower. . . .

I hope this very interesting letter will reach you safely, dearest.

I believe, love, I must be at Bristol from Saturday till Wednesday or Thursday
next. I will let you know more certain tomorrow, but answer me by return of post,
and then I can arrange accordingly. I may probably come home for Friday, and then
we return together. There is a horrible harp, upon which really and honestly somebody has every few minutes for the last *three hours* been strumming chords always
the same. . . .

Goodbye my dearest Love,

Yours,
I.K. BRUNEL.

Some of the stresses of the railway-construction period were play-
fully revealed to Charles Saunders:

I have cut myself off from the help usually received from assistants. No one can fill
up the details. I am obliged to do all myself, and the quantity of writing, in instructions alone, takes four or five hours a day, and an invention is something like a spring
of water – limited. I fear I sometimes pump myself dry and remain for an hour or two
utterly stupid. . . .

If ever I go mad, I shall have the ghost of the opening of the railway walking before
me, or rather standing in front of me, holding out its hand, and when it steps forward,
a little swarm of devils in the shape of leaky pickle-tanks, uncut timber, half-
finished station houses, sinking embankments, broken screws, absent guard plates,
unfinished drawings and sketches, will, quietly and quite as a matter of course and
as if I ought to have expected it, lift up my ghost and put him a little further off than
before.

One of the larger devils which beset Brunel and which he had van-
quished to his satisfaction was the gauge of his railway. The gauge
of four feet eight and a half inches had been arbitrarily accepted by
George Stephenson because, his son Robert explained, 'it was the
original gauge of the railways about Newcastle-upon-Tyne', referring
of course to the early horse-drawn coal-waggons. Brunel called this
contemptuously 'the coal-waggon gauge', and insisted that the Great
Western was to be run on a broad gauge 'more commensurate with the
mass and velocity to be attained'. From a practical point of view his
broad-gauge trains had great merits; but as a policy his insistence upon
a seven foot gauge was disastrous since it was clear that railways in the

One severe inconvenience of the G.W.R.'s adoption of broad-gauge track was the necessity of changing carriages at points of connection with other lines. IKB's insistence on broad-gauge, though in the end economically a mistake, was a tribute to his awareness of its engineering advantages.

Daniel Gooch (1816–89) in 1845. Already at nineteen the designer of new and more powerful locomotives, at twenty Gooch was appointed Brunel's Chief Locomotive Assistant on the G.W.R., becoming its Chairman for the last twenty-four years of his life.

rest of the country would run on standard gauge. Replying to criticisms he wrote:

The Great Western Railway broke ground in an entirely new district, in which railways were unknown. . . . [It] was therefore free to adopt its own dimensions; and none of the difficulties which would entirely prevent such a course in the north of England had any existence in the west. Consequently all the general arguments advanced . . . on the supposition of such difficulties occurring . . . are totally in-applicable to the particular case of the Great Western Railway, to which they have no reference whatever.

In the circumstances the broad gauge was one of his greatest mis-takes – not a failure of engineering but an error of policy and foresight which was quite unlike him.

It lasted for only fifty-four years before being torn up to make way for the standard gauge, though it had, in the words of an obituarist, 'done great things for English railways in its youth by setting an example of speed, weight-hauling and smooth running'.

Brunel made a brilliant choice of lasting value to him and to the railway when he brought in young Daniel Gooch as his Locomotive Assistant. This dour north-countryman while in his teens had been working for Robert Stephenson in Newcastle, and he was just under twenty-one when he joined Brunel, at a salary of £300 a year, shortly before the first trains were to run. He could not have differed more from Brunel in temperament. He left a Brunel social gathering 'disgusted with London parties, making a note in my memo. book never to go to another'. But when it came to nursing the early locomotives, developing new ones, and exploring all the potentials of a great rail-way, he was the ideal complement to Brunel.

The spirit of Brunel presides over the burial of the broad-gauge railway.

A crowd gathered on 20 May 1892 at Paddington Station to bid farewell as the last broad-gauge train, the *Cornishman*, set out on its final run to Penzance. One day later the conversion to standard narrow gauge had been effected.

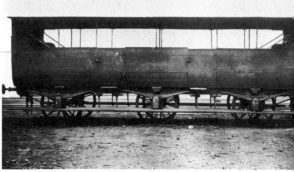

Gooch's *North Star*, originally designed for export to America, was the one dependable locomotive in use by the G.W.R. at the opening of the line to Maidenhead. She became the prototype for Gooch's later and greater broad-gauge flyers.

(*Above, right*) Train travel in the earliest days was uncomfortable for all but first-class passengers, and even they were not always well accommodated. This forbidding broad-gauge coach, twenty-seven feet long, in use about 1840–50, was an improvement over prior third-class travel, which consisted simply of space on the exposed platforms of goods trains.

(*Above, opposite*) The original G.W.R. terminus at Paddington.

(*Below, opposite*) Constrained by an order of the Thames Commissioners that his railway crossing at Maidenhead leave the towpath and navigation channel unobstructed, IKB solved his engineering problem by constructing this extraordinary bridge in which each brickwork arch has a span of 128 feet, with a rise of only 24 feet 3 inches to the crown.

His first job was to receive two locomotives Brunel had ordered to his own specifications, *Premier* and *Vulcan*. They had been built in the North of England and were delivered by canal barge to West Drayton to be put on the mile and a half of track already laid between that point and Langley. *Vulcan* made a trial run on 28 December 1837, the first locomotive to run on the G.W.R. On 8 January 1838, George Henry Gibbs, a Director whose diaries give a lively picture of the early life of the line, became acquainted with both *Vulcan* and *Premier*: 'The engines, after some delay in getting up steam, sallied forth; but the curve in the turn-out proving too sharp for them, they got off the rail two or three times, and it was an hour before they could be got on the main line. When there, however, they performed beautifully, and we had a very interesting drive.'

The significant note here was the trouble about getting up steam: for in fact both locomotives were under-boilered. Young Daniel Gooch soon found that he was expected to cope with locomotives which, owing to the conditions imposed by Brunel upon the manufacturers, were little short of monstrosities. Though Brunel had done his home-work with characteristic thoroughness – his notebooks are proof of that – these locomotives ordered for the Great Western were, in the words of Mr L. T. C. Rolt, 'the greatest and most inexplicable blunder in his whole engineering career'.

Providentially, Gooch had persuaded Brunel to acquire also *North Star* and *Morning Star* which he himself had designed (when still in his teens) for Robert Stephenson for shipment to America. Their export having fallen through, they were duly ferried on the Thames by barge to Maidenhead where they became, as soon as the track reached them, the only reliable locomotives the new Company possessed.

North Star stood at the head of the train when members of both Houses of Parliament, 'other people as for various reasons were deemed worthy of a place', Mary Brunel and a few other ladies

Rain, Steam and Speed, by J.M.W. Turner – a train of the G.W.R. crossing the Maidenhead Bridge.

assembled at the gaily decorated wooden station-building at Paddington on 31 May 1838. Gibbs wrote in his diary: 'At 11.30 we entered the carriages of the first train and, proceeding at a moderate pace, reached Maidenhead Station in 49 minutes, or at about 28 miles an hour. After visiting the works we returned to Salt Hill where a cold luncheon for about 300 was laid under a tent. After the usual complement of toasts we returned to the line and reached Paddington (19 miles) in 34 minutes, or $33\frac{1}{2}$ miles an hour.' He did not mention that Thomas Guppy was so elated by the event, and perhaps the entertainment, that he amused himself by walking along the roofs of the carriages and jumping from one to another on the way back to Paddington.

Owing to the inadequacies of the locomotives but also to flaws in the permanent way, the G.W.R. made a sorry start. In July Gibbs noted:

Went at four o'clock to Paddington and soon after news was brought us that the *Vulcan* was off the line and had sunk up to the axle. This led to an accumulation of trains and people, and in the attempt to correct the evil another engine got off the line and sank in the same way. The consequence was that many hundreds of people were disappointed, and the 4 o'clock train did not reach Maidenhead till past 10. I was so sick of the scene that I made off. . . .

But Gibbs did not desert the sorely beset Brunel. Though he saw some deficiencies in the man who was designing and creating what was to become the finest railway with the fastest trains in the world, he championed him against the heavy critical assaults which came especially from the northern Directors of the line, the 'Liverpool party' as they were called. Though he refused the chairmanship, Gibbs succeeded in dominating the board-room until such time as Brunel's line had proved itself.

Poor young Gooch became for a time the scapegoat of the loco-motive troubles, but he lived through it, forsaking a young wife to spend nights in the engine-sheds, until he began to get the locomotives of his own design. Ultimately he became Chairman of the G.W.R., a Baronet and a Member of Parliament.

The Great Western Railway was completed, in stages, by June 1841. Brunel left his mark everywhere. His famous bridge crossing the Thames at Maidenhead consisted of two of the largest and flattest arches ever built of brick. The critics said it would collapse when the staging was taken down in 1839, but it stands today, widened, to carry loads inconceivable at its birth.

Beyond Twyford, at Sonning, was the great cutting two miles long and sixty feet deep, which broke two contractors. To complete it, Brunel assumed personal control, mustering a force of 1,220 navvies and 196 horses, fighting flood and mud: the first train went through to Reading in March 1840. In the autumn of that year New Swindon was founded and laid out as a railway-works town. In 1841 the Box Tunnel was finished. When, in that year, the beflagged inaugural train steamed through from London to Bristol in four hours, the passengers were received at Temple Meads beneath the wooden hammer-beam roof – wider than that of Westminster Hall – of a station designed by Brunel, which remains one of the noblest manifestations of the Age of Steam.

Gooch was at the controls, with Brunel beside him, on the momen-tous occasion in the summer of 1842 when Queen Victoria first went by train. There was little advance notice of this event, the Company being notified on Saturday afternoon that Her Majesty would travel from Slough to Paddington on the following Monday. They had long since prepared a royal saloon which was upholstered, according to the *Illustrated London News*, 'in the rich style of Louis XV, with hanging sofas of carved wood and crimson and white silk, with paintings on the walls representing the four elements by Parris'. Both stations were hurriedly decorated, and the word spread that the Queen was at last setting the seal of her approval upon railroads in general and the G.W.R. in particular. She was received at Paddington with 'deafening' demonstrations of loyalty. To her Uncle Leopold, King of the Belgians, she wrote: 'We arrived yesterday morning, having come by the railroad from Windsor, in half an hour, free from dust and crowd and heat, and I am quite charmed with it.' Her most cherished Minister somewhat quixotically wrote: 'Lord Melbourne was sure that Your Majesty. *being fond of speed*, would be delighted with the railway.'

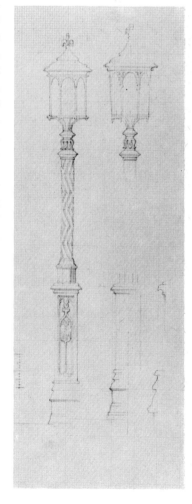

Designs from IKB's notebooks for lampposts at the Bristol station. Every detail of design and construction on the 120-mile line gave evidence of Brunel's originality and attention.

(*Top*) The bustle of departure
beneath the great arched bays of
Paddington Station.

(*Right*) IKB's sketchbook designs
for the new station at Paddington,
opened in 1854.

(*Above*) Detail of interior design for
Paddington Station, exhibiting the
exuberant mid-Victorian taste for
ornamentation.

Temple Meads Station, Bristol.
The rail-level was raised by Gothic
arches fifteen feet above ground-level
and covered by a wooden hammer-
beam roof of seventy-two feet span,
combining elegance and spaciousness.

With minor architectural changes,
the Bristol station remains today as
Brunel built it.

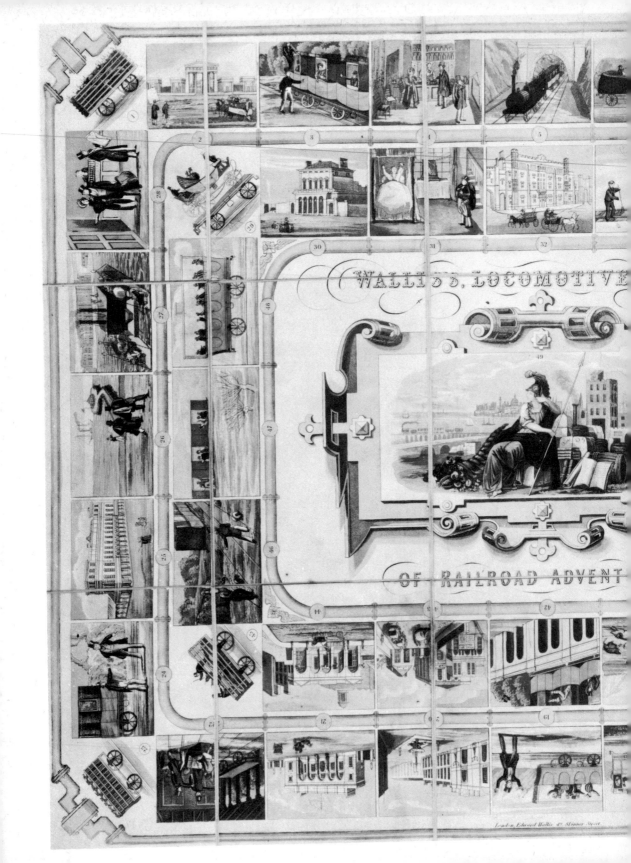

WALLIS'S, LOCOMOTIVE

OF RAILROAD ADVENT

London, Edward Wallis, 42 Skinner Street.

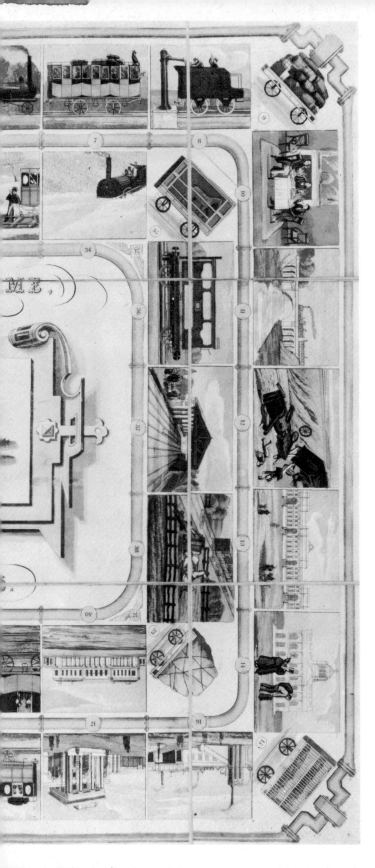

Excitements of the railroad's earliest era are pictured in Wallis's Locomotive Game. Number 32 shows the exterior of the G.W.R.'s Bristol station.

In conjunction with the new station at Paddington a hotel was opened, and Brunel added to his multifarious enterprises by taking an active hand in its direction.

The Queen began to use Brunel's railway regularly, in spite of such newspaper admonitions as that of the *Atlas*, which declared 'a long regency in this country would be so fearful and tremendous an evil that we cannot but desire, in common with many others, that those Royal railway excursions should be, if possible, either wholly abandoned, or only occasionally resorted to'.

For several years the Queen used the unimpressive Paddington terminus at Bishop's Road. In the early 1850s, with the excitement of the Great Exhibition convulsing the creative life of the country, a fitting terminus at Paddington was proposed. Brunel wrote an enthusiastic letter to the eminent architect (Sir) Matthew Digby Wyatt:

I am going to design, in a great hurry, and I believe to build, a Station after my own fancy; that is, with engineering roofs, etc. etc. It is at Paddington, in a cutting, and admitting of no exterior, all interior and all roofed in. . . . Now, such a thing will be entirely *metal* as to all the general forms, arrangements and design; it almost of necessity becomes an Engineering Work, but, to be honest, even if it were not, it is a branch of architecture of which I am fond, and, *of course*, believe myself fully competent for; but for *detail* of ornamentation I neither have time nor knowledge, and with all my confidence in my own ability I have never any objection to advice and assistance even in the department which I keep to myself, namely the general design. . . .

Are you willing to enter upon the work *professionally* in the subordinate capacity (I put it in the least attractive form at first) of my *Assistant* for the ornamental details?

Having put the question in the least elegant form, I would add that I should wish it very much, that I trust your knowledge of me would lead you to expect anything but a disagreeable mode of consulting you, and of using and acknowledging your assistance; and I would remind you that it may prove as good an opportunity as you are likely to have (unless it leads to others, and I hope better) of applying that principle you have lately advocated.

If you are disposed to accept my offer, can you be with me this evening at 9½ pm? It is the only time this week I can appoint, and the matter presses *very much*, the building must be half finished by the summer. Do not let your work for the Exhibition prevent you. You are an industrious man, and night work will suit me best.

I want to show the public also that *colours* ought to be used.

The new Paddington to which Sir Matthew Digby made a few ornamental contributions was opened by the Prince Consort in 1854. It was a tribute to Brunel's forward-looking designs that the station sufficed for the G.W.R. traffic, without extension, for more than fifty years. The Paddington Hotel opened at the same time, with Brunel, at first a Director, later Chairman of the hotel company, taking an active part in the hotel management.

That his comments on catering could be as astringent as any on engineering is evident in his letter to the refreshment-room contractor at Swindon Station: 'I assure you Mr Player was wrong in supposing that I thought you purchased inferior coffee. I thought I said to him I was surprised you should buy such bad roasted corn. I did not believe you had such a thing as coffee in the place; I am certain I never tasted any. I have long ceased to make complaints at Swindon. I avoid taking anything there when I can help it.'

'. . . I have no hesitation in taking upon myself the full and entire responsibility of recommending the adoption of the Atmospheric System on the South Devon Railway. . . .' Brunel had been appointed Engineer to the railway and made this incredibly rash statement in a report to the Directors in August 1844. The line was to connect Exeter with Plymouth providing an extension of the broad-gauge system. The fifty-odd miles offered some stiff gradients for the limited capacity of the locomotives of those days. Brunel argued that it would be cheaper to lay out a track for atmospheric traction which would climb more easily and that the running costs would be more economical. Such a system had been carrying passengers for some five months at Dalkey on the Kingstown to Dublin Railway when he made his recommendation, and he had paid two visits to Ireland to inspect it.

The system in any case had attracted him for some time. Four years previously he had attended trials at Wormwood Scrubs of an atmospheric railway patented by Samuel Clegg and the Samuda brothers. He went there not just as a spectator but with the thought that the

The vacuum tube of the London and Croydon line. A piston, attached to the bottom of the railway carriage, was pulled by suction and was allowed to travel through the tube by means of the hinged slot at the top.

(*Top*, *opposite*) The vacuum tube being laid between rails for the South Devon Atmospheric Railway. The line functioned under constant difficulty for only one year before being converted to conventional traction.

(*Centre*, *opposite*) Details of the atmospheric railway devised by the Samuda brothers and Samuel Clegg, and used by the Dublin and Kingstown Railway on its short branch line between Kingstown and Dalkey.

(*Below*, *opposite*) A passenger train of the South Devon Atmospheric Railway in operation along the sea-wall built by Brunel near the resort town of Dawlish, showing the piston carriage, vacuum tube, pumping station and disc and crossbar signals also designed by IKB.

system might possibly be applied to the gradient at Box Tunnel. The opinions of his fellow engineers had been divided. The Directors of the Dublin Railway and their Engineer, Charles Vignoles, approved and subsequently set to work, as did William Cubitt with the London & Croydon Railway. Joseph Locke and the Stephensons disapproved. Besides calling it a 'great humbug', old George Stephenson observed: 'It won't do: it is only a modification of the fixed engine and ropes . . . .' A French delegation thought well of it, and a short section of the Paris–Saint-Germain Railway operated atmospherically for some years. Brunel himself recommended it for part of the Genoa–Turin line.

Basically the atmospheric scheme, which briefly became something of a mania, consisted of a cast-iron tube laid between running rails. At intervals along the rails – three miles apart on the South Devon – stationary engines worked air-pumps which exhausted air from a section of the tube, creating a vacuum. A close-fitting piston, attached to the carriage running on the rails, placed at one end of the section of tube would be drawn, as the vacuum built up, towards the end where the air-pump was working. In Devon, ten pumping-stations were built and engines were supplied by Boulton & Watt, Rennie, and Maudslay & Field. Cast-iron tubes were supplied by George Hennett at the rate of a mile a week. The line was laid as far as Newton Abbot during 1846, when Joseph Samuda and some of his men who already had experience of working the London & Croydon line arrived in Devon. Early in 1847 the first piston carriage ran six miles out of Exeter, but already there were difficulties – mainly over delay in com-

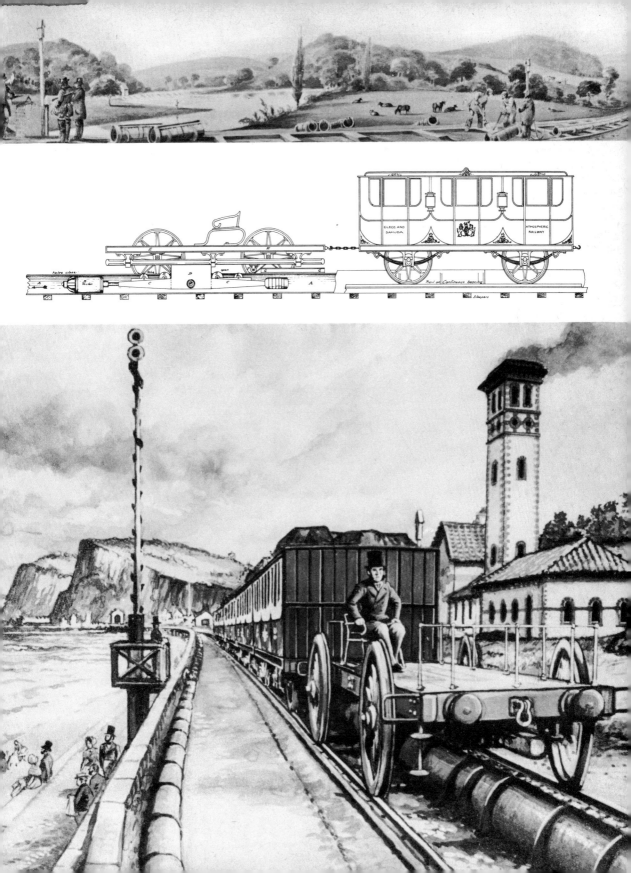

CLEGG AND SAMUDA

ATMOSPHERIC RAILWAY

Rail on Continuous bearing

Sleepers

pleting the stationary engine-houses – and in August Brunel made a statement regretting that they had not been able to open any part of the line to the public. In September things began to look expensive and it was decided not to carry the system beyond Totnes until it had proved itself.

Later that month the public service opened between Exeter and Teignmouth. At first the public was enthralled by the experience of riding so smoothly uphill without smut, smoke, dust or noise. They were soon disillusioned. The atmospheric trains refused to start, ran slow, arrived late and sometimes had to be pushed by the passengers. Everything went wrong. Extreme heat and extreme cold destroyed the leather used in the valves. As in the Croydon line, rats acquired a taste for the material after it had been treated with seal oil. Curiously enough there were also persistent failures and inadequacies in the static pumping-stations which, unlike the track mechanism and equipment, were not engineering novelties but had been constructed with their engines to Brunel's own specifications. Only eight months after the system between Exeter and Newton was opened, Brunel had to report to the Directors that the 'Atmospheric Caper', as Devonians had already dubbed it, was a total loss and that they would have to revert to conventional steam-traction. The atmospheric mania faded everywhere. In Ireland, the mile and a half track was never extended. At Croydon, nearly £500,000 was spent but within little over a year the equipment was sold for scrap.

The South Devon experiment, when it was abandoned in 1848, had cost over £426,000 of which some £50,000 was recovered from the sale of the plant. The crippled Company was eventually taken over by the G.W.R. Brunel suggested that the electric telegraph, which he had instigated between Paddington and Slough and which had been refused him in Devon on account of expense, might have enabled the pumping-stations to work more efficiently and economic- ally, generating power only when there was an oncoming train. Apart from this he fairly and squarely took the blame, declining any remuneration for his professional services as Engineer, apart from the retaining fee. Since he always put some of his own capital into his ventures, he also incurred considerable financial loss. 'This costly mistake brought down the fury of shareholders, and certainly under- mined confidence in him, for a time,' wrote his grand-daughter.

It may, at least, be said that he did not shirk his own responsibility, nor consent to an attempt to patch up the faulty system, as suggested by his directors. Once con- vinced of failure, he preferred to acknowledge it openly and return to safe ground. By substituting our now familiar material of rubber for leather, a perfectly satisfactory valve could have been obtained; but the price of rubber was then prohibitive. . . .

Against this failure in South Devon, which delayed but did not

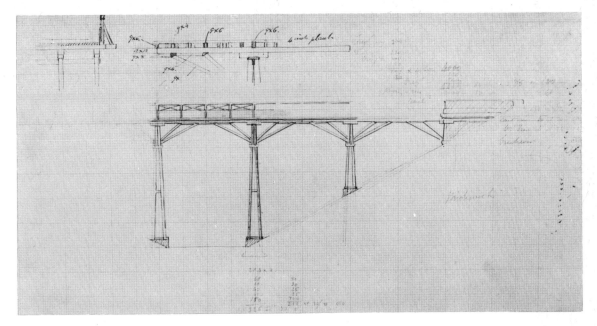

impede the progress of the railway system, may be balanced two triumphant enterprises in the West. The first was the bridge over the Wye at Chepstow, opened in 1852, bringing South Wales into direct communication with London. The second and more magnificent was the Royal Albert Bridge at Saltash completed in 1859, which extended the broad gauge into Cornwall.

Brunel had already built five splendid timber viaducts between Totnes and Plymouth. At Chepstow his crossing of the Wye was by a wrought-iron bridge which was to be the prototype for his master-piece at Saltash. When it came to working in iron Brunel's philosophy contrasted with that of his friend and rival Robert Stephenson. Where Brunel insisted on wrought iron, using it to provide flexible structures in which the load was spread, Stephenson sometimes used a com-bination of cast iron and wrought iron with disastrous results. When he favoured wrought iron, it was in braced structures, such as the Newcastle high-level bridge or his famous Britannia Bridge over the Menai Strait. In Brunel's bridges at Chepstow and Saltash the loads were transmitted through wrought-iron suspension hangers. Both bridges were subject to Admiralty requirements, the first to give clear headway of 50 feet above high water, the second to give 180 feet, with minimum openings of 300 feet.

The left bank of the Wye at Chepstow formed a limestone cliff 120 feet high; low ground, liable to flood, lay on the other side. Brunel's bridge was of a suspension type. The main span over the river, 300 feet long, was suspended from the ends of an iron tube mounted on piers rising 50 feet above rail-level. The three land spans on the right

Brunel's sixty-seven timber viaducts, constructed of economical and durable Baltic yellow pine, were among his most graceful and original designs. Unfortunately, due to the rising cost and declining quality of replacement timber, all of these structures have now vanished, masonry or iron taking their place, though the last was in use until 1934.

The railway bridge at Chepstow, replaced in 1962. Brunel was faced here not only with strict Admiralty requirements, but with the peculiar lie of the land, nearly sea-level washland on one side and a limestone cliff 120 feet high on the other.

(*Top, opposite*) His work in sinking the central piers for the Chepstow Bridge provided Brunel with the necessary experience for the even more delicate task of construction on the Royal Albert Bridge at Saltash. Here a caisson is placed to act as a coffer-dam within which the masonry pier could be built.

(*Centre, opposite*) Work in progress on the Saltash bridge. One of the main trusses is already in place, the other awaits completion of the foreshore pier before being lifted.

(*Below, opposite*) The completed bridge. The upper tubes, in the innovative oval shape Brunel preferred, are arched to equal the fall of the suspension chains.

bank, 100 feet long, were supported on piers of cast-iron cylinders. These had been weighted until they had gone down through the soft boulder-clay and penetrated a rock stratum over 80 feet below high water; they were then filled with concrete.

At Saltash Brunel, as Engineer to the Cornwall Railway, was faced with a river 1,100 feet wide and 70 feet deep at high water – with an Admiralty ruling that the fairway was not to be obstructed by scaffolding. He decided on a high-level bridge combining, as at Chepstow, suspension and tubular principles. His design was for two 455 feet spans supported by only one central pier in the river. As with every other project of his the budget weighed heavily upon him. After he had devised an ingenious and indeed dramatic method of construction and carried out trials, the Company ran short of cash and suspended operations for three years. When work was resumed, he had to cut back and budget for a single- instead of a double-track railway crossing.

The whole of the ironwork came from the Orchard Works at Blackwall on the Thames. By the Tamar a great cylinder was prefabricated then floated out into the river to be sunk in an upright position to form a huge coffer-dam. Within this the central pier was constructed. The trusses were assembled in the same way on the river-banks to be floated bodily into position. The tension chains, no doubt a good buy for the Company, were for Brunel a reminder of his first great uncompleted masterpiece. They had been purchased from the Clifton Bridge Company, which had run short of cash and stopped work a few years before.

For the floating of the first truss, weighing a thousand tons, Brunel became the centre of one of the most dramatic and yet meticulously

A conference of engineers consulting on plans for the Britannia Bridge. (Robert Stephenson, seated centre, IKB, seated far right.) Stephenson repaid Brunel's help in later years by his generous support during the crucial months of launching the *Great Eastern*.

organized engineering events of the century. He was mounted upon a platform directing the whole operation by a system of signals done with numbers and flags. He demanded absolute silence, and the dense crowds who turned out respected this. According to an eyewitness,

Not a voice was heard . . . as by some mysterious agency, the tube and rail, borne on the pontoons, travelled to their resting place, and with such quietude as marked the building of Solomon's temple. With the impressive silence which is the highest evidence of power, it *slid*, as it were, into its position without an accident, without any extraordinary mechanical effort, without a 'misfit', to the eighth of an inch.

As Brunel stepped down from the platform the band of the Royal Marines played 'See the Conquering Hero Comes'. It was an astonishing feat both of engineering and of man-management. His experience at Chepstow had helped. More significant perhaps had been the assistance he lent to Robert Stephenson when floating the tubes of his great Britannia Bridge in the Menai Strait. And all this experience was to have great relevance to the launch of the *Great Eastern* steamship later.

The Saltash Bridge was another achievement Brunel was not to finish in person. When, in 1859, the Prince Consort travelled down on the broad gauge from Paddington to name it the Royal Albert Bridge, Brunel was a dying man. He went only once to see the completed work. Unable to stand or walk, he lay on a platform truck and was drawn slowly across by a G.W.R. locomotive. It was his first and last look at his masterpiece.

Though many of the great technological advances of this century, such as aviation, owe their impetus to the pressures of war, Brunel and his contemporaries changed the face and economy of the country in a period of prolonged peace, turning Britain from a rural community to an industrial nation, themselves too preoccupied for any misgivings about the human consequences.

When the long peace came to an end in 1854 with the Crimean War, Brunel was soon in correspondence with James Nasmyth about the improvement of heavy guns. Then in 1855 he was offering the Admiralty a design for a gunboat, or floating gun-carriage, which was to have a submerged hull and be jet propelled by steam. Soon afterwards he wrote of the Admiralty: 'They have an extraordinary supply

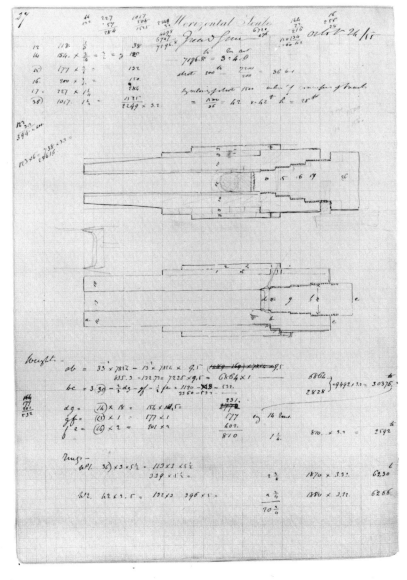

Brunel's active mind addressed itself to engineering problems of every kind. Here, a sketchbook design for a 'great gun'.

of cold water and capacious and heavy extinguishers, but I was prepared for and proof against such coarse offensive measures. But they have an unlimited supply of some *negative* principle which seems to absorb and eliminate everything that approaches them. . . .'

He came into his own when Florence Nightingale denounced bureaucracy and demanded emergency hospitals in the Crimea. The target for the fury of this famous and formidable lady was the very bureaucrat whose energies Brunel had always respected, his own brother-in-law and admired friend Sir Benjamin Hawes, who had become Permanent Under-Secretary at the War Office. Inevitably Brunel was invited to help. He replied, on the same day that he received the request, that his 'time and best exertions would be, without any limitations, entirely at the service of the Government'. This was in February 1855. In March he wrote a memorandum setting out his plans.

The conditions I considered necessary were firstly that the buildings should be capable of adapting themselves to any plot of ground (within reasonable limits), secondly, that each set of buildings should be capable of easy extension from holding 500 patients to 1,500. Thirdly, that they would contain every comfort which it would be possible to afford; fourthly that they should be very portable, and of the cheapest construction. The whole hospital will consist of a number of separate buildings all of the same size and shape, so that with an indefinite length of corridor, they may be arranged in any form to suit the ground. Each building is to contain within itself all that is necessary to an independent hospital ward-room, so that by the lengthening of the corridor and the addition of any number of their buildings, a hospital may be extended to any degree.

Twenty-three steamers bore the sections, each complete in itself, to Renkioi in May. The hospital with its modern sanitation and provision for fresh air accepted its first patients in July, and by the end of

Florence Nightingale's angry reports of conditions in the military hospitals at Scutari created a national scandal.

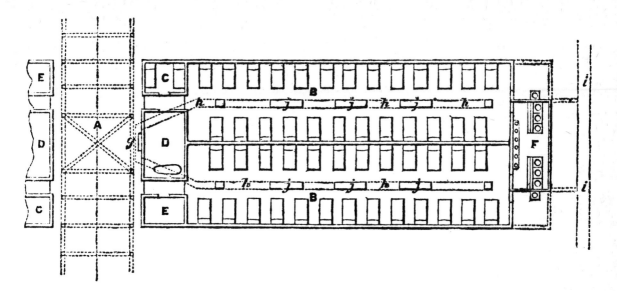

that year – only ten months after Brunel took on the job – the full quota of one thousand beds was in use. It was a complete success, though through no fault of its designer it arrived in the Crimea too late to avert the catastrophic conditions which roused such widespread indignation and immortalized Florence Nightingale. No record, alas, exists of 'The Lady with The Lamp' and 'The Little Giant', both such highly charged characters, ever having been in direct communication.

Brunel's design for a temporary hospital, with advanced sanitary facilities and excellent ventilation. Flexible in size and adaptable to varied conditions, his hospital was constructed in England and shipped for assembly to Renkioi in the Crimea.

One of the vessels carrying troops and supplies to the Crimea was the *Great Britain*, the second of Brunel's famous steamships. His first had been the *Great Western*, and the last, which was his undoing, was the *Great Eastern*. All three were sensational in their time, not only for their design, size and performance, but also for their lurid mishaps. Just as Brunel was more creative than some of his contemporary poets, he was also more in personal danger than many eminent soldiers of his time.

His was an amphibious nature though he never made any spectacular voyages or showed any ambition towards navigation. Even from his schooldays of 'making half a dozen boats', his approach towards maritime matters was always that of an engineer. This interest increased during his working life until, with the conceiving of the *Great Eastern*, it became an obsession.

His practical work on steamships began in 1835, when the Great Western Railway was being planned. At a meeting of the Directors there were complaints and misgivings about the 'enormous' length of the new line. 'Why not make it longer, and have a steamboat to go from Bristol to New York, and call it the *Great Western*?' Brunel exclaimed. There was merriment, but the joke in fact had a cutting-edge. Brunel and his devoted friend Thomas Guppy sat up that night

William Patterson of Bristol, in whose dockyards both the *Great Western* and the *Great Britain* were constructed. A strong admirer of Brunel, he indignantly attacked Scott Russell's later attempts to discredit him.

discussing the possibility of crossing the Atlantic by steam. Brunel was logical and consistent. He maintained that it was possible to design with the materials and skills then available a steamship which could carry enough coal to cross the Atlantic or indeed for even longer distances. It was a matter of size and proportion. This thought came at a time when the steamship had been nudging its way into maritime trade for more than two decades. The Atlantic had already been crossed by vessels fitted with steam-engines: the *Savannah*, from New York in 1810; and the *Royal William*, in 1833 from Canada. In 1815 a steam-ship had begun to ply between Liverpool and Glasgow. In 1826 a 'leviathan steamship', the *United Kingdom*, was built for the London–Edinburgh route – the coastal trade being of great importance before the advent of railways.

By that year the General Steam Navigation Company had extended its activities beyond home waters and was running a regular steamer service between London, Brighton, Portsmouth and Lisbon, Oporto and Gibraltar. Though ocean-sailing vessels and the great clippers were to be built for another forty years, steam was already established when Guppy and a committee of railway Directors formed the Great Western Steamship Company to turn Brunel's 'extension' from Bristol to New York into a reality. Significantly, two other organizations were forming about the same time – in London, the British and American Steam Navigation Company; and at Liverpool, the Transatlantic Steamship Company. Britain's three great ports were competing for the Atlantic.

In July 1836 work was started in William Patterson's shipyard at Bristol on Brunel's design for the steamship. The hull was oak-built, larger than that of any other steamship of the period, and the engines ordered from Maudslay's were of unprecedented size. The work was well under way when Dr Dionysius Lardner appeared in Bristol to address the British Association and prove, with his customary display of phoney statistics, 'the inexpediency of attempting a direct voyage to New York'. He calculated that 2,080 miles was the longest run any steamer could make: 'at the end of that distance she would require a relay of coals'. Brunel was in the audience and rose to confute the Doctor. This historic and no doubt diverting encounter unfortunately went unrecorded.

Brunel was more concerned with the rival enterprises. The Liverpool company had purchased an uncompleted 1,150 ton vessel, the *Liverpool*, but as she was not ready they chartered the second *Royal William*, launched in 1837 and intended to work in the Irish Channel. The London company decided not to wait for the *British Queen*, which they were having built in the Thames for the Atlantic run; instead they purchased the *Sirius*, a 700 ton vessel also recently launched for Anglo-Irish traffic, and were having her hastily fitted out for the transatlantic race – for that was what it had become.

Brunel revelled in such competitive situations. His letters to Guppy during this period reveal an exuberant concern with the fortunes of his competitors – particularly the *Sirius*. The *Royal William* was soon recognized to be a late-starter.

The Cork Steam-Ship Company's
STEAM SHIP
SIRIUS
700 TONS, 320 HORSES POWER.

Little more than half the size of the *Great Western*, the *Sirius*, built for the Anglo-Irish service, was modified to compete in the transatlantic race. On 22 April 1838 she became the first British steamship to reach New York.

(*Right*) Three hundred guests attended a special luncheon in her main saloon when, with hope and excitement, the *Great Western* was launched in 1837. But she had still to spend more than six months in London to take on her engines and to have her interior fittings completed.

(*Below*) After a voyage of only fifteen days – and one day behind the *Sirius* – the *Great Western* arrived in New York to share in the acclamations: 'cheering rose from the shore . . . loudly and gloriously, as though it would never have done'.

(*Opposite*) Following her initial triumph, the *Great Western* became the first steamship to engage in regular transatlantic service, completing seventy-four crossings in the course of her career. Brunel's first great liner, she was 236 feet long and had been conceived as the ocean-going extension of the G.W.R.

After inspecting the progress of Maudslay's engines in April 1837, Brunel wrote: 'I cannot help still feeling some hopes that we may effect that most important object of performing the voyage across the Atlantic this Autumn.' This was altogether too sanguine. The ship was launched, amid acclamation, at Bristol in July 1837, but still had to sail round to the Thames to have her engines fitted and her excitingly elaborate interior completed. Thousands of Londoners went down the river to Blackwall to wonder at her black hull 236 feet long, and some were privileged to share this glimpse by a contemporary writer of the interior.

The saloon of this vessel is 75 feet in length, longer than any other steam ship or vessel in the World, and 21 feet wide, except where there are recesses on each side when it is 34 feet and 9 feet high clear of the beam, which is increased by the lantern light. It will be needless to enter into a minute description of all the ornamental paintings, decorations, etc., which are so lavishly expended on this saloon, but it will suffice to say that all the taste and skill of the first rate upholsterers, decorative and landscape painters, etc., etc., have been employed on it.

The writer may well have been cut short in the midst of his etceteras. There was increasing bustle to get the *Great Western* out of the Thames and back to Bristol, ready for her maiden voyage to America. The heat was on – the little *Sirius*, only half the size of the *Great Western*, was also being fitted in the Thames.

Brunel, Guppy and Captain Claxton were aboard the *Great Western* supervising her final trials on 28 March 1838, when the *Sirius* captained by Lieutenant Roberts, R.N. sailed off down the river with forty passengers bound for New York, but with a coaling stop at Cork. Not until 31 March could Lieutenant James Hosken, R.N., Master of the *Great Western*, with Brunel and other Directors on board, give chase towards the English Channel, making for Bristol to pick up passengers and supplies and to start the Atlantic trip. They reckoned they still had a good chance against the *Sirius*.

For two hours they steamed steadily down the estuary on a clear spring morning; then, just off the Nore, their high hopes were smothered in sudden clouds of acrid smoke. Deficient lagging beneath the base of the funnel had caused the deck beams and under side of the deck planking to catch fire. The Chief Engineer George Pearne described his own actions in the log.

The fore stoke-hole and engine room soon became enveloped in dense smoke, and the upper part in flames. Thinking it possible the ship might be saved, and that it was important to save the boilers, I crawled down, after a strong inhalation of fresh air, and succeeded in putting on a feed plunger and opening all the boiler feed cocks, suffering the engines to work to pump them up, as the steam was generating fast from the flames round the upper part of the boilers.

To help Pearne, Claxton groped his way down to the boiler-room.

As he stood in dense smoke at the foot of the ladder playing a hose on the fire, he was struck to the floor by a heavy object falling from above. Picking himself up, he discerned a man's body, inert, the head already almost submerged in water from the hoses. He yelled aloft for a rope and had the body hauled up.

It was Brunel. Still unconscious, he was laid out on a sail on deck, while Hosken ran the ship aground near Canvey Island, and the fire was brought under control. Intent on fighting the fire himself, Brunel had rushed to the ladder to join Claxton below. One of the upper rungs, partially burned through, had given way and sent him hurtling down some eighteen feet, probably to his death if Claxton had not been there to break his fall. In great pain, but urging them to carry on at all costs, he was taken ashore at Canvey Island where he was immobilized for several weeks – characteristically sending a detailed list of instructions to be carried out while the ship coaled and victualled at Bristol.

She sailed on 8 April, short of passengers, for news of the fire had caused many cancellations. Four days earlier, the *Sirius* had left Cork, and after nineteen days at sea the little craft arrived off New York on 22 April with less than fifteen tons of coal left in the bunkers. She docked on the following morning. On the afternoon of the same day the *Great Western* anchored off Sandy Hook with two hundred tons of coal still in hand, only fifteen days and five hours out from Bristol. She had lost the honour of being the first steamship across, but she was the first one built specifically for the job and her trip, with seven apprehensive passengers, founded a dynasty of ocean greyhounds. The 'Liverpool people' did not manage to get the *Royal William* across from the Mersey to Sandy Hook till July of that year.

New York's acclamation of the *Sirius* was duly extended to the *Great Western* and one of her passengers left this record: 'Myriads were collected, boats had gathered round us in countless confusion, flags were flying, guns were firing, and cheering rose from the shore, the boats and all around loudly and gloriously as though it would never have done. It was an exciting moment, a moment of triumph.'

The American Press described the *Great Western*'s engine as 'awful to behold, so immense is it' and the ladies' boudoir as 'a love of a spot'. Her performance immediately encouraged bookings and there were sixty-eight passengers for the return trip to Bristol, which took fourteen days. Her return was greeted with bell-pealing and flag-flying. The *Bristol Mirror* declared that 'the joy and pleasure announced by all classes upon her arrival has been unequalled in the city for many years, and they almost stand upon a level with the tidings from the Nile, Trafalgar Bay, and the plains of Waterloo'. After this initial excitement the *Great Western* settled into a routine of successful service, making seventy-four Atlantic crossings during her career.

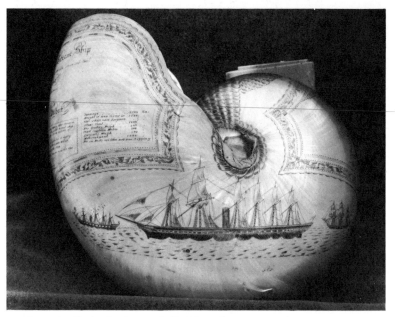

An engraved nautilus shell celebrating the *Great Britain*, with details of her dimensions and launching.

Viewers were undoubtedly gratified by the ease of the *Great Britain*'s launching from dry dock under the auspices of Prince Albert. But similar crowds were, a few years later, to mar the completely different task of launching the *Great Eastern*.

Though she had almost killed her designer at the outset, her performance immediately proved his points about long-range steamships. Indeed, before she had completed her second trip Brunel was already engaged on her successor which was to be sensational. In its early stages characteristically dubbed the *Mammoth*, this was later altered without too much modesty to the *Great Britain*.

At first another wooden ship had been envisaged and the timber for it actually bought. Brunel, however, persuaded his Directors that this was to be an iron ship, and his building committee consisting of Guppy, Claxton and himself made a special study of a small experimental iron steamer, the *Rainbow*, which called at Bristol in 1839. The following year there was another visitor, the *Archimedes*, a small auxiliary schooner having the novelty of a screw-propeller. Brunel studied this too and sent Guppy off on a trip to investigate its performance at sea. When Guppy reported favourably, the work on the great paddle engines was scrapped and their designer, Francis Humphrys, was ordered to provide screw engines in their place. It was a ruthless decision and it actually killed Humphrys. 'He was a man of the most sensitive and sanguine constitution of mind,' wrote Nasmyth. 'The labour and anxiety which he had already undergone, and perhaps the disappointment of his hopes, proved too much for him and a brain fever carried him off after a few days' illness.'

When tenders to build the greatest iron hull in the world – 322 feet long – failed to materialize, the Great Western Steamship Company went into business itself, buying and reconstructing Wapping Wharf at Bristol. After the switch from paddle to screw and the death of

An engraving to commemorate the launching of the *Great Britain*, IKB's novel iron-hulled, screw-driven liner, on 19 July 1843.

On the day of the launching a banquet for six hundred guests was held in the smithy of the dockyard alongside the ship.

Humphrys, the Company more rashly committed itself to the construction of the engines at Bristol. Brunel had confronted his supporters with a task involving new materials, a new method of propulsion and a new type of engine. To Guppy he wrote: 'If all goes well, we shall all gain credit, but *quod scriptum est manet*; if the result disappoint anybody, my written report will be remembered by everybody, and I shall have to bear the storm.'

There were the usual financial difficulties, accentuated by the fact that they were doing work at Bristol which should have been done by established marine engineers in established yards. It all took longer than expected, but there was a day of triumph in July 1843 when the ship was named and launched by the Prince Consort. This was indeed a remarkable day for Isambard Brunel: he, with Daniel Gooch, was on the footplate of the locomotive which drew the royal train from Paddington – and the G.W.R. was duly proclaimed in the *Illustrated London News*, as 'the longest independent line completed in this country, so all its appointments are in keeping with this superiority. . . . The vastness of construction throughout the line entitle it to the rank of "Grand", and even "Gigantic".'

Aboard the *Great Britain* there was a banquet for six hundred people – many of them with an appetite sharpened by the 7 a.m. start from Paddington. A local reporter noted: 'The demolition of the various delicacies proceeded quietly, and it was gratifying to observe that the west country air appeared to have in no wise disagreed with the Royal appetite.'

Nevertheless, after this triumphant launching, the ship's arrival in the Thames was delayed for more than a year. In December 1844 there were difficulties in getting her away from Bristol. 'She stuck in the lock; we *did* get her back,' wrote Brunel. 'I have been hard at work all day altering the masonry of the lock. Tonight, our last tide, we have succeeded in getting her through; but, being dark, we have been obliged to ground her outside, and I confess I cannot leave her till I see her afloat again, and all clear of her difficulties.'

Finally, in the spring of 1845, the ship lay in the Thames astonishing London and Queen Victoria. The *Great Britain* was one-third longer than any battleship in the Queen's Navy. She carried sixty-four state-rooms, with a music-room and boudoirs and twelve hundred yards of specially woven scarlet and purple Brussels carpet. The Queen viewed all this but was spared descent to the engine-rooms. A working model had been specially made so that Brunel could explain the ship's workings to his Queen in the Grand Saloon.

Her maiden voyage was between Liverpool and New York in August 1845. The second voyage that year showed she was deficient in steam-raising power, and during the winter she was modified. After two successful voyages the following year, she left Liverpool on her

RIVER THAMES
JAN. 28. 1845.
WE THE UNDERSIGNED PASSENGERS,
ON BOARD THE GREAT BRITAIN STEAM SHIP,
ON HER EXPERIMENTAL VOYAGE FROM BRISTOL
TO LONDON HAVING WITNESSED HER PERFORMANCES
DURING A STIFF GALE AND A HEAVY SEA DO EXPRESS
OUR CONVICTION OF HER GREAT LENGTH BEING NO
DETRIMENT TO HER EXCELLENT SAILING QUALITIES
& HER SEA-WORTHINESS, AND OF THE GREAT ADVANTAGE
OF THE APPLICATION OF Mr SMITHS SCREW, AS ALSO OUR
SENSE OF THE SKILL, ATTENTION, AND URBANITY OF HER
COMMANDANT LIEUT. HOSKEN, R.N.
SIGNED S. LUSHINGTON CAPT. R.N. A. FAIRBROTHER M.D.
W.H.G. LANGTON, J. REYNOLDS R.Y.S, JOHN REYNOLDS,
I. WHITE, J.H. BROWN, C.M.S, E.J. MAUDE, C.E, C. WEST,
J.M. SUNLEY, W.G. EVANS, W. ROUGHSEDGE, W. COOK,
H.J. MILLS, T.D. TAYLOR, G.J. POWELL, J. WALTER,
E.J. MAYBURY J. LOVELL, J.G. POWELL,
C. HILL, E.C.S, A. HONEYWELL, W. HERNIMAN,
J. HAMMONDS, C.E, P.P. BAILEY C.E
G. PYCROFTE, M.R.C.S.

Having encountered unusually heavy seas in the trial run from Bristol to London, where her fitting out was to be completed, the *Great Britain* received this testimonial from her passengers.

fifth voyage in September 1846 with a hundred and eighty passengers, the largest number that had been carried up to that time by any transatlantic steamer. They were not, however, to reach their destination. Owing to a misreading of lights on the Isle of Man or to a compass failure, the *Great Britain* ran aground on rocks in Dundrum Bay in Ireland. 'We have, indeed, been in fearful peril. . . .' wrote a lady passenger afterwards.

All was confusion; men and women rushed from their berths, some threw themselves into the arms of strangers; one could with difficulty stand. Mr——'s first words to me were, 'I think there will be no loss of life, but the ship is gone.'

What fearful words on such a dark night! Oh! I cannot tell you of the anguish of that night! The sea broke over the ship, the waves struck her like thunder claps, the gravel grated below. There was the throwing overboard of coal, the cries of children, the groans of women, the blue lights, the signal guns, even the tears of men, and amidst all, the Voice of Prayer, and this for long dark hours. . . . At dawn we were lowered over the ship's side and carried on shore in carts of seaweed manure, and Mrs—— and I lay upon the floor of an Irish cabin where we found plenty of bread, some bacon, and divided an egg among three. There was an efficient coastguard, but at one time the Irish assembled in such numbers that we feared a riot. To my astonishment and gratitude all the luggage was saved.

As the Company teetered towards bankruptcy, the ship lay with ten feet of water in her hold and no efforts could get her off that autumn – the autumn of Brunel's atmospheric railway project in South Devon. When at last in December he went across to Ireland, he got straight down to the need for immediate protection of the vessel. As he wrote to Claxton:

I was grieved to see this fine ship lying unprotected, deserted and abandoned by all those who ought to know her value, and ought to have protected her, instead of being humbugged by schemers and underwriters. . . . The result . . . is that the finest ship in the world, in excellent condition, such that £4,000 or £5,000 would repair all the damage done, has been left, and is lying, like a useless saucepan kicking about on the most exposed shore that you can imagine, with no more effort or skill applied to protect the property than the said saucepan would have received on the beach at Brighton. . . .

As to the state of the ship, she is as straight and as sound as she ever was, as a whole. . . . I told you that Hosken's drawing was a proof, to my eye, that the ship was not broken: the first glimpse of her satisfied me that all the part above her 5 or 6 feet water line is as true as ever. It is beautiful to look at, and really how she can be talked of in the way she has been, even by you, I cannot understand. It is positively cruel; it would be like taking away the character of a young woman without any grounds whatever.

The ship is perfect, except that at one part the bottom is much bruised and knocked in holes in several places. But even within three feet of the damaged part there is no strain or injury whatever. . . . What are we doing? What are we wasting precious time about? The steed is being quietly stolen while we are discussing the relative merits of a Bramah or a Chubb's lock to be put on at some future time! It is really shocking. . . .

He immediately devised a system of protection which consisted mainly of faggot bundles which preserved the ship during the

(*Opposite*) The hulk of the *Great Britain* in 1969, being towed from her graveyard at Sparrow Cove, Falkland Islands, the first step in her triumphant return to Bristol for preservation.

At first abandoned after running aground in Dundrum Bay, the *Great Britain* was finally protected against further damage by 'a mass of strong faggots lashed together with iron rods . . . like a huge poultice'.

remainder of that winter. In the following summer she was refloated and towed to Liverpool for repair. Her adventure proved the value of iron construction and fully vindicated Brunel's design.

It also proved too much for the Company, which was forced into liquidation. The *Great Western* was acquired by the Royal Mail Steam Packet Company. The *Great Britain*, bought by Giggs, Bright & Company of Bristol and Liverpool, was re-engined and refitted for the Australian trade. She steamed out of Liverpool in 1852 on her first voyage to Melbourne with 630 passengers on board. She made thirty-two voyages in twenty-three years, taking some sixty-five days each way. She was conscripted for service in the Crimea, carrying 1,650 troops and 30 horses: she spent six months trooping during the Indian Mutiny. Though in her long years of success she was out of Brunel's hands, she more than vindicated all his calculated risks.

Her very powers of survival are a tribute to his abilities. In 1882, aging and retired from the Australian run, she was sold again. Her new owners wanted her only as a sailing-ship to carry coal to San Francisco and bring back wheat. They therefore removed her engines and, for reasons unknown, sheathed her iron hull entirely in wood. In 1886, on her forty-seventh voyage out, she encountered terrific storms round the Horn and was beaten back to the safety of the Falkland Islands where she ran aground. After being declared a total loss she lingered ignominiously as a wool and coal hulk. In 1937 she was towed to Sparrow Cove, three and a half miles from Port Stanley, deliberately holed and declared to be a Crown Wreck. But in Britain public concern and private subscription enabled a team to carry out a rescue operation. One hundred and twenty-seven years to the day after her launch she was brought back to her own dry-dock in Bristol, having passed beneath Brunel's Clifton Suspension Bridge, to be acclaimed as a memorial to his part in pioneering the revolution from sail to steam.

An enormous shadow loomed over the latter years of Brunel's life and work – that of the *Great Eastern*, launched at prodigious cost in 1858. Her 692 feet length was not to be surpassed for nearly half a century, nor her displacement of 22,500 tons exceeded until the ill-fated *Lusitania* was built in 1906. She had six masts, five funnels, a twenty-four foot screw, paddles and sixty-five hundred square yards of sail. She was designed to carry four thousand passengers – almost twice as many as the Cunarder *Queen Mary*. She was a sensational success as a technical achievement and a colossal failure as a financial operation. She killed her designer.

She was born of the climate of optimism emanating from the Great Exhibition of 1851. The prestige of engineers had never stood so high: and among this new élite, enhanced always by the enthusiasm of the

The Crystal Palace, rebuilt in Sydenham after the close of the Great Exhibition, was flanked by water-towers (one visible here at far right) designed by Brunel.

The Machinery Court at the Crystal Palace, showing in the background the huge hydraulic press used in raising the tubular sections of Robert Stephenson's Britannia Bridge.

Prince Consort, I. K. Brunel's name was held in high esteem. 'Even to shake hands with one so remarkable was a thing to be remembered for a lifetime,' was the attitude of at least one of his contemporaries. In spite of the failure of the atmospheric railway and the sale of his two steamships, he remained very much on top of the world. He applauded Paxton's Crystal Palace and was influenced by it in his own designs for Paddington Station. When it was removed from Hyde Park to Sydenham he designed the two water-towers which flanked it there. While the Exhibition in London was enhancing the feeling that there was nothing short of flight which the nineteenth-century engineer could not achieve, news was coming through of fresh discoveries of gold in Australia. With the already increasing emigration, this stimulated a boom in the Australian shipping trade. So as the *Great Britain* set out on her first voyage to Australia for her new owners, there appeared in Brunel's notebooks, among drawings of the new Paddington Station, sketches for an 'East India Steamship. . . . Say 600 ft × 65 ft × 30 ft'. These were first notes for the design of a steamer which would be big enough to carry her own coals for a trip to Australia and back. As this idea grew towards obsession Brunel found what he took to be the perfect partner to give it reality – and he made the greatest personal misjudgment of his career by choosing – John Scott Russell.

He had met Scott Russell on committees connected with the Great Exhibition. On the face of it, the man, who was about his own age, had the right qualifications. He was a Fellow of the Royal Society, Vice-President of the Institute of Naval Architects and of the Institution of Civil Engineers. He was a brilliant, practical marine engineer with his own yard at Millwall on the Isle of Dogs. The fact that he was a villain was not apparent to Brunel until much too late. Even now it is difficult to explain Scott Russell's motives for the deception and villainy which impeded the launching of the *Great Eastern* and shortened Brunel's life.

Gold-prospecting in Australia in the 1850s. Increased emigration and trade stimulated IKB to his most ambitious maritime scheme – a ship big enough to carry her own coals for a trip to Australia and back.

John Scott Russell, F.R.S. Brunel's choice of Russell as partner in his last great undertaking constituted 'the greatest personal misjudgment of his career'.

Early notebook sketches for the *Great Eastern*.

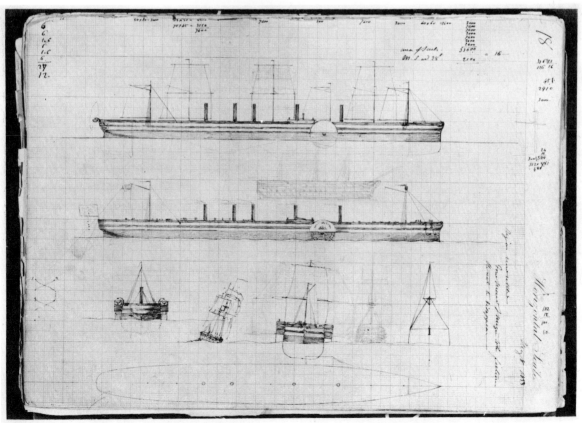

At Scott Russell's suggestion the scheme for the great ship was offered to the Directors of the Eastern Steam Navigation Company who were at that time in need of some new stimulus, for the British Government had granted their mail contract exclusively to the P. & O. The Directors favoured the idea and while capital was being raised there was virtually a reconstruction of the Company. Brunel placed a number of his nominees as Directors and put up a lot of his own money. 'I never embarked in any one thing', he wrote at the time

to which I have so entirely devoted myself, and to which I have devoted so much time, thought and labour, on the success of which I have staked so much reputation, and to which I have so largely committed myself and those who were disposed to place faith in me; nor was I ever engaged in a work which from its nature required for its conduct and success that it should be entrusted so entirely to my individual management and control. . . .

The Directors accepted this dictatorial attitude. So, for the time being, did Scott Russell who was tendering for the job. Brunel had estimated, very optimistically, the cost of the ship to be some £500,000. Scott Russell's tender surprisingly was for only £377,200, which he even offered to reduce by more than £100,000 if a further contract was placed with him for a sister ship.

In December 1853 Scott Russell's contract was signed. It 'provided for the construction, trial, launch and delivery of an iron ship of the general dimensions of 680 ft between perpendiculars, 83 ft beam and 58 ft deep according to the drawings annexed signed by the engineer, I. K. Brunel'.

It would appear that Brunel was in absolute command of the whole operation – and he may well have imagined this himself. In actual fact he was financially tied up by the resources of the Company, and he was handing over to Scott Russell immense powers of passive resistance. Russell was in charge of the hardware, Brunel of the paper. Though it was not at once evident, that division of power was to prove fatal.

Russell agreed at the outset to have the ship built in a dock. It is amazing that anyone, least of all Brunel, should have taken Scott Russell seriously when he quoted £8,000 to £10,000 for the cost of a dry-dock. But soon afterwards, pleading the difficulty of finding a suitable site, he shrugged off the whole idea. The only alternatives were launching end-on or sideways-on. To launch at right angles to the river, which is only about a thousand feet wide at Millwall, Brunel pointed out, could mean a gradient of one in fifteen and bring the forepart of the ship forty feet in the air. Better a controlled sideways launch down an inclined way into the river; for this Brunel conceived the design for a mechanical slip, fitted with wheels or rollers that would lower the huge mass and float her off on the tide. This equipment was turned down as altogether too expensive, an economy which was to cost dear.

Meanwhile the keel was laid in July 1854; the hull was to be built up from the ground and consist of thirty thousand iron plates, the average weight of each being one-third of a ton. Three million rivets were to be hammered in by hand. The screw engines were built by Watt in Birmingham, the paddle engines by Scott Russell at Millwall. As the work began, its fame went before it. A sample of the thousands of speculative words written about the *Leviathan* (as she was often called before taking the water as the *Great Eastern*) was this flight of jingoism:

This country has in 'Leviathan' the strongest, swiftest, and most terrible of ships if war instead of commerce should be her destiny. . . . Ten thousand men could be landed at any point of danger, ready to step from deck to field. . . . Here we have a floating fortress, camp and parade ground in one, to make one and indivisible our world-wide empire. Our insularity from our colonies will be annihilated, and we shall acquire a military position corresponding to the extent of our dominion and the numbers and greatness of our race. . . . It is consolatory to know that private enterprise has added so enormously to the national means of self-defence in England, and thus contributed to her general safety. This mighty fabric, indeed, will not talk, but it will act – its act being a month's voyage from India to Australia. . . .

The screw engines for the *Great Eastern*, constructed by James Watt & Company, were largely built to Brunel's original designs and specifications. They had four cylinders each, of seven feet diameter, with a nominal horsepower of sixteen hundred.

Yet all was not well. Scott Russell was insisting on a free launch, stating that a controlled launch would be outside his contract and much more expensive. Apart from this basic disagreement the actual work was awry. In April 1855 Brunel wrote to Russell: 'I begin to be quite alarmed at the state of your contract – four months are gone and I cannot say that even the designs are completed or even sufficiently settled to justify a single bit of work being proceeded with – we shall get into trouble.' In August Brunel switched to banter – with an edge to it.

I have tried gentle means first, I must now strengthen the dose a little. If you do not see with me the necessity of shaking off suddenly the drowsiness of sleep that is upon us and feel it so strongly that like the sleepy man just overcome with cold you feel that unless done instantly you are lost – In fact unless, as I say, on *Monday next* we are busy as ants at ten different places now untouched I give it up – but you will do it.

The four paddle-engines, built by Scott Russell, were of conventional design but unprecedented size. Special furnaces were required to complete the paddle-shaft, which was at the time the largest forging ever attempted, weighing over forty tons.

In December he wrote: 'I cannot stand any longer the anxiety I have felt ever since we commenced the ship as to her launching and having now calculated myself her weight and centre of gravity at time of launching I must have her centre of flotation and this your people can do better than mine.'

Scott Russell's lack of co-operation in 1855 was disquieting. In 1856 it became flagrant. It was evident too that his original estimate for the hull and paddle engines had been totally irresponsible. He had, with a good deal of cajolery, obtained payment of all but £40,000 of the sum. Yet three-quarters of the hull was still unfinished. He owed for much of the iron and was deeply in debt all round. In February 1856 he discharged all the men and for nearly four months the ship-yard remained silent. There were creditors' meetings. At one time Scott Russell offered to continue the work for the fantastic sum of £15,000 a month. Finally – though this was by no means the last of him – he repudiated his contract: 'It is not proposed to continue the construction of the leviathan vessel of the Eastern Steam Navigation Company, the Contract passing to the Directors. Up to the present time no loss has been sustained in connexion with the steamer; but if the work is continued it would, no doubt, exhibit an unfavourable result.'

There was no alternative but for the Company to take over the work. Brunel assumed control on 22 May 1856, with a note to his Chairman announcing: 'We propose to commence work on Monday morning.' However, when the yard came to life again, he was far from holding the absolute control he had once dreamed of, and the Company was paying through the nose for every day's work. Yet the great ship began to take shape and the wonder of the world grew. 'The voyager up and down the Thames has noticed with astonishment the slow growth of a huge structure on the southern extremity of the Isle of Dogs', wrote the *Quarterly Review*.

At first a few enormous poles alone cut the sky-line and arrested his attention, then, vast plates of iron, that seemed big enough to form shields for the Gods, reared themselves edgeways at great distances apart, and as months elapsed, a wall of metal slowly rose between him and the horizon.

She is destined to carry eight hundred first class, two thousand second class and one thousand and two hundred third class passengers, with a ship's company making a total of four thousand and four hundred people. . . . From side to side of her hull, she measures 83 ft., the width of Pall Mall. She could just steam up Portland Place, with her paddles scraping the houses on each side. . . . We might also dwell for a moment upon her mighty larder, or draw a comparison between her and the Ark (which by the way had not half her capacity) as she receives on board her flocks and herds, to furnish fresh meat for the passage. But we believe we have said enough to enable those who have not visited the rising edifice to realize the vast extent of the latest experiment in ship-building.

Built to convey four thousand passengers, or ten thousand troops in an emergency, the ship seemed to many people a white elephant. One cartoonist provided this solution to the question of 'What to do with the *Great Eastern*' and proved, by the way, prophetic.

Brunel (second from right) and others watch preparations for a renewed effort to move the inert ship.

One of the checking drums to control the slide of the hull towards the water. During the first launch attempt the stern cradle moved with unexpected speed, taking up the slack chain and causing the checking drum to revolve. Inattentive workmen, still leaning on the handles, were spun into the air and one was killed.

The hull of the *Great Eastern*, having been moved more than two hundred feet from the construction site, awaits high tide before the final launching attempt.

This was all very well, but it represented some twelve thousand inert tons – the largest dead weight man had ever tried to move – which had to be slid sideways into the Thames. In October 1857, when she was ready for launching, the *Great Eastern* lay 330 feet from the surface of the water at high tide. To get her down on the incline of one in twelve Brunel had devised slipways with make-do apparatus, including ships in the river to control the launch. It was the best that could be done on the money and, like the arrangements he had made for the dramatic floating into place of the Saltash Bridge, its operation called for discipline and exact timing. 'I propose to commence operations', he wrote in a memo to all concerned,

about two hours before high water and to endeavour to get the ship down as quickly as I can into the water and down to within about thirty-six feet of the bottom of the ways. . . . Provided the mechanical arrangements should prove efficient, the success of the operation will depend entirely upon the perfect regularity and absence of all haste or confusion in each stage of the proceeding and in every department and to attain this, nothing is more essential than *perfect silence*. I would earnestly request, therefore, that the most positive orders be given to the men not to speak a word and that every endeavour should be made to prevent a sound being heard, except the simple orders quietly and deliberately given by those few who will direct.

But on 3 November 1857 the discipline demanded, more especially the *perfect silence*, were wiped out by the fame of the event and by the folly of Brunel's Directors who sold thousands of tickets. 'Men and women of all classes', wrote a reporter,

were joined together in one amicable pilgrimage to the East, for on that day, at some hour unknown, the *Leviathan* was to be launched at Millwall. . . . For two years, London – and we may add, the people of England – had been kept in expectation of the advent of this gigantic experiment, and their excitement and determination to be present at any cost, are not to be wondered at when we consider what a splendid chance presented itself of a fearful catastrophe.

As at Saltash, Brunel personally directed the launch from a platform, by means of an intricate and well-rehearsed system of signals. He stood little chance, however, against the hubbub of the crowds invading every inch of the yard. At last the cry went up – 'She moves', and the monster slid a few feet down the slipways. Then came disaster. The crew manning a drum cable, distracted by the crowds and inattentive, were hit by the spinning of their winch. One man was killed outright. Brunel stopped the launch. In the words of his son: 'The whole yard was thrown into confusion by a struggling mob, and there was nothing to be done but to see that the ship was properly secured, and to wait till the following morning.'

The next day did not see the *Leviathan* launched. From that November until the last day of the following January 1858, she lay on the foreshore being inched sporadically towards the tideway. Once the initial impetus had been lost it was going to take a prodigious amount of force and ingenuity to get her into the water. It soon became apparent that this would take weeks rather than days. Luckily for the morale of all concerned, the fact that it might take months of exhaustive effort did not occur to them.

But for the time being the wonder of it all was shattered. A prodigy which had awakened the interest of the civilized world and could startle it, like the Great Exhibition itself, was suddenly immobilized. It was not only the momentum of a vast hulk of metal but that of a proud dream which had been lost. There had been too much publicity, too many chances taken. It had been the multitude that had stopped the launch, not the furious Little Giant on the launching-platform; yet he whose disappointment had been greatest was the one who would be made to pay for it. A fickle Public was disenchanted: a hostile Press made the most of a great opportunity for denigration. 'Why do great companies believe in Mr Brunel?' wrote *The Field*, in those days not confined to rustic matters. 'Is it because he really is a great engineer? If great engineering consists in effecting huge monuments of folly at an enormous cost to shareholders, then is Mr Brunel surely the greatest of engineers. . . .'

The writer then took a swipe at the 'bore', the Thames Tunnel 'which our uncles and aunts used to look upon as the eighth wonder of the world', but which had become a 'shilling sight for holiday-makers'. Next he dealt with the Box Tunnel. 'Mr Brunel could . . . have made a better line by going round the hill. But no: another monument to his vanity was needed, and so *through* it he went. . . .'

The assault upon the operations at Millwall opened by pointing out that the cost had been £1,000 for every foot 'along which the unwieldy monster has been forced'. After reciting the hopes raised and dashed by fellow scribes on the daily Press, the writer closed on a note of gloomy prophecy. 'We have no doubt that by this time the shareholders have grown somewhat sick of hope, and distrustful of Mr Brunel's confidence; nor can we regard the whole affair otherwise than as a striking lesson to public companies for the future.'

The public was not wholly unsympathetic to Brunel and suggestions, many of them from the lunatic fringes, poured in. There was the man who would levitate the vessel by pumping her full of gas. There was the one who struck a personal note: 'I am a thirteen stone man, I laid myself flat on a table, six men, three on either side, put their forefingers, at respective distances, and lifted me with ease, and could have carried me round the room – I suggest the idea, hoping it may be useful in moving your Monster difficulty.'

There were suggestions about manpower: 'I would put one or two thousand men on board the ship and give them a signal by trumpet alarm to unite in jumping and I should not fear but the vibration

Brunel (far right) on the launching platform awaiting the final, successful attempt to launch the *Great Eastern* in January 1858.

created would be effectual, together of course with your other appliances, to set the machine in motion. . . .'

Among those who thought of explosives was this one: 'It strikes me that if several large guns were loaded with powder only and placed alongside the "Leviathan" and fired simultaneously with the hydraulic rams and other machinery in operation that the explosion would give an impulse to the Ship and cause her to move off easily.'

Then there were those in favour of using natural resources: 'Could not 50 Navigators (with materials ready) stop the tide above Chelsea, and then raise the Thames Water for you?'

Brunel answered and kept all such suggestions and these extracts have been made from a bundle carefully preserved among his papers.

Meanwhile it became abundantly clear that what was needed was more and more power. This was confirmed by Robert Stephenson who emerged very touchingly to stand by Brunel during this period of prolonged crisis. Like Brunel, Stephenson was an ailing man and his visits to the Millwall shipyard were a great tax on his strength, as some of his correspondence reveals: 'I shall remain at home all to-morrow with the view of being ready for Monday morning (if the weather be at all tolerable) at Millwall, for my mind is really continually there.' He had also got the measure of Scott Russell. 'Never mind Russell or the papers. I shall always be at hand happen what may, to aid and do everything in my power without shirking any responsibility if need be.'

In this and many other ways Robert Stephenson's presence gave confidence to Brunel. The country was scoured for presses. Among them was that used for lifting the tubes of Robert Stephenson's Britannia Bridge. By January 1858 the total force amounted to some fifty-five hundred tons, equal to nearly half the weight of the inert hull. Still the assault on the ship brought its disasters, as reported by *The Times.*

It was something unheard of in the history of mechanics. In fact the accident to a windlass, when a side of its massive iron drum was crushed like a nut, was not only never known to occur before, but until yesterday such a breakage was considered almost impossible. Through the sides of a hydraulic ram, ten inches in diameter, the water was forced through the pores of the solid iron like a thick dew, until the whole cylinder ripped open from top to bottom with a noise like a dull underground explosion. The iron of this cylinder averaged six inches in thickness and stood a

Richard Tangye and one of his hydraulic presses which were called into service by Brunel to provide added power. These machines performed so well that the business of the Tangye brothers soon grew and they later said, 'We launched the *Great Eastern* and she launched us.'

THE GREAT EASTERN STEAM SHIP.
SCREW, PADDLE AND SAIL. FOUR DECKS.
WOULD ACCOMMODATE 10,000 TROOPS.

692 F. LONG. 83 F. WIDE.
HEIGHT OF HULL 60 F.
24,000 TONS BURDEN
2,600 HORSE POWER

A medal commemorating the launching of the *Great Eastern*, after months of heart-breaking effort and bankrupting expense.

pressure upward of twelve thousand pounds per square inch before it gave way. The massive cast-iron slab against which the base of another ram rested was split like a board, but this of course was a mere bagatelle among the other mishaps, which are not only expensive in themselves but by the delays they give rise to, occasion an expenditure in which the cost of the repair is a mere item.

That abortive attempt on 5 January, described above, was followed by more successful efforts, until on 14 January the forward cradle had travelled 197 feet and the after cradle 207 feet toward the water. Finally on Sunday, 31 January the *Great Eastern* floated off on the tide and was shepherded across the river to moorings at Deptford. She carried Brunel with his wife and family across the water. He had gone without sleep for more than sixty hours. His health was broken. His Company was in ruins. The ship had cost £732,000 and was not remotely ready to put to sea.

Once again he was left with an uncompleted masterpiece, and from the Press and the public the jeers mingled with the cheers. This time his resilience was gone. He lacked the physical strength to cope with a vast financial problem in what happened to be a year of commercial slump. In answering an invitation about a month after the launch, he

(*Opposite*) For a year after she was finally set afloat, Brunel's 'great babe' remained at moorings, little more than a hull, while finances were sought to complete her outfitting.

His health undermined by exhaustion, and suffering from Bright's disease (nephritis), Brunel was ordered to winter in Egypt where he 'relaxed' by renting a Nile sailing-boat, travelling upriver as far as the Aswan Falls whence, after an excursion to Philae by donkey, he proceeded in a lighter craft to ascend the rapids.

(*Opposite*) The spaciousness and sumptuousness of the *Great Eastern* were without parallel. First-class staterooms, capable of being enlarged to accommodate whole families, contained a wash-basin, concealed bath with hot and cold water, a dressing-table and a rocking-chair. The Grand Saloon, flanked by a balcony (seen here), was sixty-three feet long, forty-seven feet wide and fourteen feet high.

wrote: 'I am quite unable to come, I would not trouble you with an invalid's journal . . . being weak, I am regularly floored with a concatenation of evils.'

Two months later he was ordered abroad on holiday. Characteristically he took some work with him – designs for the Eastern Bengal Railway. Meanwhile his ailing Company was seeking to raise some £172,000, which was the estimate for fitting out the ship. There was talk of putting her up to auction as she lay, a hulk at Deptford. During his absence Queen Victoria visited the ship and was dismayed not at its condition but at the state of the river, reported to Brunel in a letter from his sister-in-law: 'Wm Reid says, on going down to the *Great Eastern*, he took the boat and it was dreadful, the water a thick black liquid, and the smell beyond description. The Queen, he says, smelt her nosegay *all the time*; the sight was beautiful, and she and her party remained an hour on board.' There was a scheme to persuade the Government to buy the ship for trooping, but in spite of the royal interest the idea was turned down.

When Brunel returned in September there was talk of a new company flotation, and by November the Great Ship Company was formed to acquire the hull of the ship for £165,000 and fit her out for sea. Brunel was appointed Engineer.

As he worked out detailed specifications his health began to give way again, and this time it became known that he was seriously ill with what was subsequently called 'Bright's disease' – one of his doctors being in fact Dr Bright. He was ordered to spend the winter in Egypt and was away until the following May 1859. During this

absence tenders for the fitting out of the ship were sent in. Incredibly, the one favoured by the Directors was that of John Scott Russell, and by the time Brunel returned he was already at work.

How Scott Russell had so swiftly resurrected his resources and his reputation remains to this day something of a mystery. For Brunel the man's success and his unctuous behaviour were an almost intolerable burden. It was impossible for engineer and contractor to work together without suspicion and mutual distrust. In spite of his continuing weakness and aware that his disease was mortal, Brunel recklessly expended himself. He was not only concerned with the newly installed engines but with supervising and checking every detail of equipment. Mirrors, Utrecht velvet furnishing, crimson silk *portières* – everything had to be passed by him. In the midst of it all he managed to travel down to Saltash for his only look at his nearly completed bridge.

By August the Gothic decoration of the Grand Saloon was finished, and members of the Lords and Commons were invited for a dinner on board. As the ship neared completion, the jeers receded and once again work was impeded by the presence of celebrities and thousands of visitors. Brunel himself met few of these. He was by this time too ill and too concerned with technicalities. He declined the invitation to the Parliamentary dinner but at the same time wrote to one of his people: 'Let me know when you work engines next; I should like to attend.' He still regarded Scott Russell's work with misgivings, but Russell himself was glorying in the limelight. A pamphlet issued on board, for sale to visitors, stated that 'the merit of the construction of the ship and her successful completion is owing entirely to the untiring energy and skill of Mr Scott Russell.'

At the beginning of September Brunel selected cabins for himself and Mary for the maiden voyage, and early on the morning of 5 September he went on board where his photograph was taken against one of the funnels. Within seconds of his posing he collapsed with a stroke and was carried ashore. He was taken home to Duke Street. As the *Great Eastern* moved off without him the Press declared: 'no ship ever went to sea carrying with her so much of the goodwill and interest of the nation.'

On 7 September the *Great Eastern* moved down to the Nore. On the morning of 9 September she steamed out into the Channel, majestically working up to thirteen knots while crowds on the coast and in small ships stood by to watch her pass. Messages were signalled back to the bed of her designer in Duke Street that all was well. Then, as she was passing Dungeness Light just after six o'clock that evening, the great ship seemed to explode. 'The forward part of the deck appeared to spring like a mine, blowing the funnel up into the air,' reported the *Times* man.

The torn funnel jacket on deck after the explosion.

There was a confused roar amid which came the awful crash of timber and iron mingled together in frightful uproar and then all was hidden in a rush of steam. Blinded and almost stunned by the overwhelming concussion, those on the bridge stood motionless in the white vapour till they were reminded of the necessity of seeking shelter by the shower of wreck – glass, gilt work, saloon ornaments and pieces of wood which began to fall like rain in all directions.

Through no fault in Brunel's design, too much steam had been allowed to build up in the feedwater heaters serving the paddle-wheel boilers. Their explosion would have destroyed a lesser ship, but using the screw-propeller engines, the *Great Eastern* was still able to steam into Weymouth. There her six dead stokers and her shaken distinguished passengers were landed, and she was laid up for repair, not to sail again until the following year.

At Duke Street the news of the disaster could not be indefinitely withheld from Brunel. He lingered for only a few days, his spirit broken. On 15 September he summoned enough strength to call to each of his family by name, then died. His friend Daniel Gooch wrote: 'By his death the greatest of England's engineers was lost, the man with the greatest originality of thought and power of execution, bold in his plans but right. The commercial world thought him

(*Overleaf*) 'The forward part of the deck appeared to spring like a mine . . . the awful crash of timber and iron mingled together in frightful uproar and then all was hidden in a rush of steam . . . glass, gilt work, saloon ornaments . . . began to fall like rain in all directions.'

extravagant; but although he was so, great things are not done by those who sit down and count the cost of every thought and act.'

The *Morning Chronicle* mourned: 'Brunel was the right man for the nation, but unfortunately, he was not the right man for the shareholders.'

The *Great Eastern* lived for just over thirty years, an uneasy, restless, mostly luckless monster, first as a loss-making transatlantic passenger-ship, then for a period enjoying worthwhile success as a cable-laying craft, then towards the end as a showboat at Liverpool.

What went wrong with the great ship, conceived so splendidly in the notebooks just enriched with the designs of Paddington Station? Was it not that often-disastrous lag between practical conception and technical performance which afflicted so many of Brunel's schemes? His ideas were sometimes revolutionary, often original, usually sound. His ability to promote them and to persuade others was exceptional. He was articulate and expressed himself in practical terms. He possessed both vision and knowledge in a world which needed such qualities and was developing the resources to use them. But the resources were not always developed enough; the finance was not always forthcoming; the available skill was not always sufficient.

The most successful period of the *Great Eastern*'s ill-fated career was spent as a cable-laying ship, the only one then afloat large enough to contain in her hold the requisite two thousand miles of cable.

In the High Court of Justice,
CHANCERY DIVISION
Mr. JUSTICE CHITTY.

BETWEEN MARK EAGLES MARSDEN for himself and all other the Holders of the A or First
Series of Debentures of the GREAT EASTERN STEAM SHIP COMPANY LIMITED .... *Plaintiff*

AND

FREDERICK NEWTON Sydney King George and THE GREAT EASTERN STEAM SHIP COMPANY
LIMITED ... ... *Defendants*

PARTICULARS AND CONDITIONS OF SALE

Of the Steam Ship GREAT EASTERN which will be SOLD BY AUCTION by Mr. CHARLES
WALFORD KELLOCK with the approbation of His Lordship MR. JUSTICE CHITTY the Judge to whom this Action
is assigned pursuant to the Order therein dated the 21st day of May 1885 at Lloyds Captains' Room Royal
Exchange London E.C. on the 28th day of October 1885 at Half-past 2 o'clock in the afternoon
if not previously disposed of by private treaty.

Particulars and Conditions of Sale with copies of the Inventories may be had gratis of MESSRS. C. W. KELLOCK
& Co. Brokers of Walmer Buildings Liverpool of their Agents MESSRS. GEORGE KAY & Co. 73 Cornhill London
E.C. of MR. HENRY DEVER of 4 Lothbury London E.C. Chartered Accountant the Receiver and Manager in
the said Action and of MESSRS. GREGORY ROWCLIFFES & Co. 1 Bedford Row London Solicitors

PARTICULARS.

The celebrated and magnificent Iron Paddle and Screw Steamship

GREAT EASTERN

22,927 TONS BUILDER'S MEASUREMENT;

18,915 TONS GROSS, 13,344 TONS NETT REGISTER;

Built on the Thames from designs and under the personal superintendence of the eminent Engineer Isambard Brunel, by the celebrated
firm of Scott Russell & Co., in 1858.

Her paddle engines which are 1000 horse-power nominal are by Scott
Russell & Co., and have recently been re-packed. Her screw engines
which are 1,600-h.p. nominal are by James Watt & Co. of Birmingham.
These engines and boilers have recently been thoroughly repaired and
cleaned.

This splendid vessel carries an enormous cargo as well as having great
space for 1st 2nd and 3rd. class passengers, and attains a very high rate of
speed.

Dimensions :—Length, 679.6ft.; breadth, 82.8ft.; depth, 60ft.

NOW LYING AT MILFORD HAVEN,
Where she can be inspected.

After her fourth cable-laying
operation in 1872, the *Great Eastern*
remained for twelve years unused,
rusting at the dock in Milford Haven.
Still the world's largest ship, she was
put up for auction in 1885 and sold
for £26,200.

Visions could be obscured by circumstances or bent out of true. Thus
the *Great Eastern* was never used, as Brunel intended, for massive
movement of people and goods to Australia. The Suez Canal opened
and channelled off the Far Eastern and Australasian trade. Those
four thousand passenger-berths were never used for the Atlantic run:
the great ship missed all the emigration traffic, her managers being
mistakenly obsessed with the luxury trade. Brunel created the prototype liner for the age which was to come. In the three decades following his death, she was a wonder, drawing crowds everywhere she
touched, but never profitably, satisfactorily used – except for the cable-
laying for which she had not been built.

Still, there is not much failure in the Brunel story – and his own acceptance of it was so ready – that there could be some temptation to agree with his contemporary detractors, such as *The Field* scribe, to label him as a megalomaniac who thought and talked big and occasionally, more by luck than by judgment, brought it off. This would be a superficial judgment. A deeper look reveals him, in failure and in triumph, as the master of the prototype, the practical prophet of technological innovation. He talked because he needed to persuade and command; he took risks because he sometimes lacked resources and finance. He dared to dream, but he demanded and revered skill.

In his world versatility was treated with respect, not with the suspicion later engendered by an age of specialists. His prodigious range of interest and activity was applauded by his fellows and by his sometimes fickle Public. His tunnels, bridges, railways, stations, ships, docks, water-towers, and the tools he devised to go with them, not forgetting the forceps for his own throat, dazzled, challenged, captivated the Victorian world. We are left in this century, to which he surely belongs as much as to his own, still awestruck by the personality and achievement of the poet-engineer they called the 'Little Giant'.

Chartered as a floating fairground and amusement park – and, incidentally, as a mammoth advertisement for Lewis's department stores – the *Great Eastern* embarked on her last adventure in Liverpool.

Worn by disease and leaning on his cane, Brunel on a final tour of inspection the day before sailing posed for this photograph. In a few minutes he collapsed and was carried ashore.

CHRONOLOGY

1769 Marc Isambard Brunel born, 25 April, in the village of Hacqueville, Normandy, the son of prosperous farmers.

1786 Enters the French Navy, sails to West Indies.

1792 In Paris. Forced to flee because of his royalist sympathies, joins loyalist guard in Rouen where he meets Sophia Kingdom, daughter of a Plymouth naval contractor, and they fall in love.

1793 Marc Isambard escapes after failure of royalist insurrection in Normandy, arrives in New York, 6 September.

1793-8 Travels in America, submits prize-winning design for new Congress Building in Washington, becomes American citizen, and is appointed Chief Engineer of New York.

1799 Leaves America, 20 January, for England, with designs for block-making machinery, meets Henry Maudslay who agrees to construct his machines. His designs accepted by the Royal Navy, marries Sophia, 1 November, and they settle in Portsea.

1799-1806 Block-making machinery under construction.

1806 Isambard Kingdom Brunel born, 9 April. Family moves to Chelsea, Marc acquires sawmill at Battersea.

1807-14 Manufactures machine-made boots for army. Government work at Chatham Dockyard.

1814 Peace after Waterloo ends boot business, leaving vast surplus stock and heavy debts. Sawmill ruined by fire.

1818 Invents and patents tunnelling shield.

1820 IKB to France, aged fourteen, to complete his education.

1821 Marc Isambard arrested for debt, imprisoned May-July, released after obtaining grant of £5,000 through intercession of Duke of Wellington.

1822 IKB returns from France, aged

sixteen, begins work in his father's office.

1824 Thames Tunnel proposed, Marc Isambard appointed engineer, family moves to Blackfriars.

1825 Tunnel work begins.

1826 Marc Isambard ill, IKB becomes engineer in charge of tunnel works.

1827 First flooding of tunnel, 18 May, work resumes in November.

1828 Second disastrous flooding of tunnel, 12 January. IKB injured, recuperates at Brighton and at father's home in Blackfriars. Tunnel work stops, 'gaz' experiments begin.

1829 IKB commissioned to carry out drainage works at Tollesbury, Essex, visits Continent, enters first Clifton Bridge competition.

1830 Second Clifton Bridge competition, IKB's design chosen.

1831 Clifton Bridge construction begins in June, suspended after Bristol riots in October.

IKB completes observatory in Kensington for Sir James South, is commissioned to undertake new dock works at Monkwearmouth, Sunderland, travels extensively in England.

1832 Electioneers in support of his brother-in-law, Benjamin Hawes, victorious radical candidate for Lambeth in the parliamentary elections. Prepares detailed report of needed improvements in Bristol docks.

1833 Bristol dock works. Preliminary survey for proposed G.W.R.

Opens offices at 53 Parliament Street.

1834 Thames Tunnel work resumes, Monkwearmouth dock work, much reduced in scope, begins.

1835 Beamish takes over as Thames Tunnel engineer, new activity starts on Clifton Bridge, extensive railway work in progress. Great Western Steamship Co. forms.

1836 Marriage to Mary Horsley, moves to Duke Street, Westminster. Railway work continues, *Great Western* under construction.

1837 *Great Western* launched. Gooch joins G.W.R.

1838 Isambard III born, first child of Mary and IKB. *Great Western* fire delays departure, ship sails on 8 April for maiden voyage to New York. First section of G.W.R. opens to Taplow. Designs for *Great Britain*.

1839 G.W.R. opens to Twyford, work on *Great Britain* begins.

1841 G.W.R. opens whole line, London to Bristol, Marc Isambard receives knighthood.

1843 Thames Tunnel opens, Swindon railway works completed, *Great Britain* launched in Bristol by Prince Consort. IKB swallows coin.

1844 Bristol and Exeter Railway opened, IKB recommends atmospheric system for South Devon.

1845 Increasing conflicts over broad and narrow gauge. *Great Britain* sails on maiden voyage to New York.

1846 Parliament passes Gauge Act, spelling eventual doom to IKB's broad-gauge rails. *Great Britain* runs aground off Ireland, Cornwall Railway approved.

1848 Work commences on Saltash bridge, Atmospheric Railway, a failure, dismantled.

1849 Marc Isambard dies.

1852 Chepstow Bridge opens. First sketches for *Great Eastern*.

1854 Work on *Great Eastern* begins in partnership with Scott Russell.

1855 Designs and oversees construction of prefabricated hospital for use in Crimea.

1856 Russell bankrupt, crisis in construction of *Great Eastern*.

1857 Launch attempts begin.

1858 Launch at last successful, new company forms to undertake completion of *Great Eastern*. IKB, his health failing, winters in Egypt.

1859 Royal Albert Bridge at Saltash completed, *Great Eastern* explodes on maiden voyage. IKB dies, 15 September.

BIBLIOGRAPHY

Beamish, Richard, *Memoir of the Life of Sir Marc Isambard Brunel*, London, 1862

Beaver, Patrick, *The Big Ship: Brunel's Great Eastern – A Pictorial History*, London, 1969

Brunel, Isambard, *The Life of Isambard Kingdom Brunel, Civil Engineer*, London, 1870 (reprinted, London, 1971)

Brunel's Tubular Suspension Bridge over the River Wye, Chepstow, n.d.

Day, John R. and Wilson, B.G., *Unusual Railways*, London, 1957

Dugan, James, *The Great Iron Ship*, London, 1953

Gladwyn, Cynthia, 'The Isambard Brunels', *Proceedings of the Institution of Civil Engineers*, London, 1971

MacDermot, E.T., *History of the Great Western Railway*, 2 vols, London, 1927–31

Noble, Celia Brunel, *The Brunels, Father and Son*, London, 1938

Noble, Humphrey, *Life in Noble Houses*, Newcastle, 1967

Pudney, John, *Crossing London's River*, London, 1972

Rolt, L.T.C., *Isambard Kingdom Brunel*, London, 1957 (reprinted, Harmondsworth, 1970)

SS Great Britain, The Illustrated London News, n.d.

LIST OF ILLUSTRATIONS

ing by Samuel Colman, 1836. City Art Gallery, Bristol

The Clifton Suspension Bridge as it was before resumption of building in 1860. City Art Gallery, Bristol

32 Clifton Suspension Bridge. Photo National Monuments Record

33 Benjamin Hawes; mezzotint by Edward Goodall after Henry Briggs, 1838. British Museum, London

Soldiers attacking Bristol rioters, 1831; lithograph, 1833. City Art Gallery, Bristol

34 Railway conveyances from Liverpool to Manchester; aquatint published by Ackermann, 1834. Photo Science Museum, London

35 George Stephenson; woven silk picture. Crown copyright. Science Museum, London

37 Isambard Kingdom Brunel; mezzotint after John Horsley, c. 1838. British Rail. Photo Public Record Office, London

38 Box Tunnel; lithograph by John C. Bourne from his *The History of the Great Western Railway*, 1846

39 Offices of the Great Western Railway Co. in the Strand, London, 1906. British Rail. Photo Public Record Office, London

42 Notice of a Public Meeting about the proposed Great Western Railway. British Museum, London

The Reverend Hawtrey; lithograph by Charles Baugniet, 1854. British Museum, London

43 Making a cutting on the Great Western Railway; watercolour by George Childs, 1841. Photo Science Museum, London

44 North Dock, Sunderland. Photo Sunderland Museum

45 Mary Horsley; painting by John Horsley. Reproduced by kind permission of the executors of the estate of the late Sir Humphrey Noble, Bart. Photo Desmond Tripp Studios Limited

Isambard Kingdom Brunel; painting by John Horsley, probably in 1848. City Art Gallery, Bristol

46 Elevations of Watcombe Park as proposed; drawings from Brunel's Office, 1854. Bristol University. Reproduced by kind permission of the Trustees of Brunel Manor

47 Lady Holland in the Library of Holland House; mezzotint by S. R. Reynolds after Charles R. Leslie. Kensington and Chelsea Public Libraries

John Calcott Horsley; engraving by M. Jackson. British Museum, London

Isambard Kingdom Brunel's offices, 18 Duke Street, London; sepia drawing. Great Western Railway Museum, Swindon. Photo Ray Gardner

48 Brodie's forceps. Reproduced by courtesy of the Royal College of Surgeons of England

49 Charles Saunders; painting. Great Western Railway Museum, Swindon. Photo Ray Gardner

51 Box-Moor Embankment; lithograph by John C. Bourne from his

London and Birmingham Railway, 1839. Guildhall Library, City of London

Aerial view of New Swindon; watercolour by Edward Snell, 1849. Great Western Railway Museum, Swindon

52 The Earl of Carnarvon; engraving by Robinson after Walker. British Museum, London

54 Daniel Gooch, 1845. Photo Science Museum, London

'The Break of Gauge at Gloucester'; engraving from *The Illustrated London News*, 6 June 1846. Victoria and Albert Museum, London. Photo Eileen Tweedy

55 'Burial of the Broad Gauge'; pen and wash drawing by Linley Sambourne for *Punch*, June 1892. British Rail. Photo Public Record Office, London

The last broad-gauge through train leaving Paddington, 20 May 1892. Photo Science Museum, London

56 The *North Star*, 1837, as rebuilt in 1854. Photo Science Museum, London

A broad-gauge coach, 1840–50. Photo Science Museum, London

57 Paddington Station; lithograph by John C. Bourne from his *The History of the Great Western Railway*, 1846. Guildhall Library, City of London

Maidenhead Bridge; lithograph by John C. Bourne from his *The History of the Great Western Railway*, 1846. Great Western Railway Museum, Swindon. Photo Ray Gardner

58 *Rain, Steam and Speed*, painting by Joseph Mallord William Turner, exhibited 1844. National Gallery, London

59 Designs for lampposts for Temple Meads Station, Bristol; pencil drawings by Isambard Kingdom Brunel from his *Great Western Railway Sketchbook no. 11*. University of Bristol

60 *Paddington Station*, painting by William Powell Frith, *c.* 1862. Royal Holloway College, Surrey

Entrance to the Offices, Paddington Station; engraving from *The Builder*, 1855. Guildhall Library, City of London

Designs for Paddington Station; pencil drawings by Isambard Kingdom Brunel from his *Large Sketchbook no. 3*. University of Bristol

61 Temple Meads Station, Bristol; lithograph by John C. Bourne from his *The History of the Great Western Railway*, 1846: Guildhall Library, City of London

Temple Meads Station, Bristol. Photo National Monuments Record

62–3 'Wallis's Locomotive Game of Railroad Adventures', *c.* 1840. Photo Science Museum, London

64 Paddington Hotel; watercolour. Great Western Railway Museum, Swindon. Photo Ray Gardner

66 Air cylinder from the London to Croydon Atmospheric Railway, 1845–46. Crown copyright. Science Museum, London

67 View of the South Devon Atmospheric Railway; watercolour,

1848. Photo Science Museum, London

Elevation and longitudinal section of an atmospheric railway, *c.* 1844. Crown copyright. Science Museum, London

Atmospheric Railway passing along the sea-wall at Dawlish; watercolour after R.B. Way. Great Western Railway Museum, Swindon. Photo Ray Gardner

69 Design for Sonningham Timber Viaduct; pen drawing by Isambard Kingdom Brunel from his *Great Western Railway Sketchbook no. 9*. University of Bristol

70 Chepstow Tubular Suspension Bridge; engraving from the *Illustrated London News*, 24 July 1852. Photo by courtesy of David Lewis and Ivor Waters

71 Saltash bridge after the sinking of the central cylinder, October 1854; lithograph. Great Western Railway Museum, Swindon. Photo Ray Gardner.

Saltash bridge under construction, 1858. Photo Science Museum, London

Saltash bridge. Photo Science Museum, London

72 Conference of engineers at the Menai Straits Bridge; mezzotint by James Scott after John Lucas, 1858. Victoria and Albert Museum, London. Photo Eileen Tweedy

73 A great gun; pen drawing by Isambard Kingdom Brunel, 1855, from his *Large Sketchbook no. 9*. University of Bristol

74 Florence Nightingale in Scutari Hospital; lithograph after William Simpson from his *The Seat of War in the East*, 1855-56. British Museum, London

75 Section and plan of Renkioi Hospital; engraving from Isambard Brunel's *The Life of Isambard Kingdom Brunel*, 1870

76 William Patterson. City Museum, Bristol

77 The *Sirius*; lithograph by George Atkinson, (1837). Photo Science Museum, London

78 Launch of the *Great Western* from William Patterson's yard, 19 July 1837; painting by Arthur W. Parsons. City Art Gallery, Bristol

Arrival of the *Great Western* off New York, 23 April 1838; engraving. Museum of the City of New York

79 The *Great Western*; aquatint by R.G. Reeves after Joseph Walter, 1840. Photo Science Museum, London

82 The *Great Britain*; engraving on a nautilus shell. National Maritime Museum, Greenwich

Poster for the launch of the *Great Britain*, 19 July 1843. City Museum, Bristol

83 Launch of the *Great Britain*, 19 July 1843; lithograph after Thomas Dunhill, 1843. City Museum, Bristol

Banquet celebrating the launch of the *Great Britain*; from the *Illustrated London News*, 29 July 1843. Victoria and Albert Museum, London. Photo Eileen Tweedy

85 Medal commemorating the trial of the *Great Britain* from Bristol to London, 26 January 1845. British Museum, London

86 The *Great Britain* in Dundrum Bay; painting by J. Walker, 1847. Photo Science Museum, London

87 The *Great Britain* being towed on a pontoon to Port Stanley, Falkland Islands, 1969. Photo Associated Press

89 Crystal Palace, Sydenham, with one of the water-towers designed by Isambard Kingdom Brunel; photographed probably by Philip H. Delamotte, *c.* 1855. Victoria and Albert Museum, London

The Machinery Court at the Great Exhibition; engraving from the *Illustrated London News*, 20 September 1851

90 Forest Creek, Mount Alexander; lithograph by George F. Angas

91 John Scott Russell. Photo Science Museum, London

Designs for the *Great Eastern*; pen drawings by Isambard Kingdom Brunel, 1853, from his *Large Sketchbook. Steam Ship*, 1852–54. University of Bristol

93 James Watt and Co.'s screw engines for the *Great Eastern*; engraving. Brunel University Library

94 John Scott Russell's paddle-engines for the *Great Eastern*; engraving. Brunel University Library

96 'The *Leviathan* Casino'; lithograph, 1857–58. Brunel University Library

John Scott Russell [?], Henry Wakefield, Isambard Kingdom Brunel and Lord Derby awaiting an attempt to launch the *Great Eastern*, 1857. Brunel University Library

97 The drum cable used for the first launch attempt of the *Great Eastern* at Millwall, 1857. Institute of Mechanical Engineers

The *Great Eastern* at Millwall before the final launch attempt, January 1858. Brunel University Library

100 Isambard Kingdom Brunel and others at the launching of the *Great Eastern*, January 1858. Brunel University Library

101 Richard Tangye beside one of the Tangye hydraulic rams used for the sixth attempt to launch the *Great Eastern*, December 1857. Brunel University Library

102 Medal commemorating the *Great Eastern*, 1858. British Museum, London. Photo Ray Gardner.

103 The *Great Eastern* towed across the Thames; lithograph, *c.* 1858. Brunel University Library

104 Temple at Philae; lithograph after David Roberts from his *Egypt and Nubia*, 1846–49. Weinreb and Douwma Ltd

105 A stateroom on the *Great Eastern*; engraving from the *Illustrated London News*, 27 August 1859. Brunel University Library

Balcony in the Grand Saloon on the *Great Eastern*. Brunel University Library

107 Funnel and jacket of the *Great Eastern* after the explosion, September 1859. Photo Science Museum, London

108–9 Explosion of the *Great Eastern*, September 1859; lithograph. Brunel University Library

110 The Prince of Wales in the cable tank of the *Great Eastern*; lithograph after R. Dudley from William H. Russell's *The Atlantic Telegraph*, first published 1866. Weinreb and Douwma Ltd

111 Auction Notice for the *Great Eastern*, October 1885. Brunel University Library

112 A handkerchief with the *Great Eastern* printed on it by *Lewis's Great Eastern Exhibition Co. Ltd*, late 1880s. Brunel University Library

113 Last photograph of Isambard Kingdom Brunel on board the *Great Eastern*, 5 September 1859. Brunel University Library

INDEX

Page numbers in italics indicate illustrations